The GREAT LEAP

Face-to-Face with Initiation and Change

HANS KORTEWEG
HANNEKE KORTEWEG-FRANKHUISEN
JAAP VOIGT

HAZELDEN®

INFORMATION & EDUCATIONAL SERVICES

Hazelden
Center City, Minnesota 55012-0176
1-800-328-0094 (Toll free U.S., Canada, and the Virgin Islands)
1-651-257-1331 (Fax)
www.hazelden.org

De grote sprong: Gaan in vertrouwen ©1996 by Servire
The Great Leap: Face-to-Face with Initiation and Change
©1998 by Hazelden Foundation

First American edition published by the Hazelden Foundation
by arrangement with Servire

Library of Congress Cataloging-in-Publication Data

Korteweg, Hans.
   [Grote sprong. English]
   The great leap: face-to-face with initiation and change /
   Hans Korteweg, Hanneke Korteweg, and Jaap Voigt.
    p. cm.
Includes bibliographical references.
ISBN: 1-56838-193-X
1. Life change events. 2. Life cycle, Human.
I. Korteweg, Hanneke. II. Voigt, Jaap. III. Title
BF637.L53K6713   1998   98-28978
155.9--dc21   CIP

Translated by Klaas van der Sanden
Book design and typesetting by Spaulding & Kinne
Cover design by David Spohn

Editor's note

In the works cited section, "my translation" refers to quotations translated by
Klaas van der Sanden.

Contents

How small that is, with which we wrestle,
what wrestles with us, how immense;
were we to let ourselves, the way things do,
be conquered *thus* by the great storm,—
we would become far-reaching and nameless.

— R. M. Rilke, "The Man Watching"

Introduction

In ancient Celtic times, whoever wanted to enter the order of the Druids had to submit to a long and intensive training. After an apprentice in this training had learned everything humanly possible, he would be subjected to the great test. In a small rudderless boat, with no sail or oars, he was entrusted to the sea and left to the mercy of the elements, which would enact his fate upon him. It was up to him to stay awake spiritually and to remain trustful, while totally unable to control his circumstances. Only he who passed this test and was guided back to shore by the stream of life was admitted to the order.

It is a mark of all initiation rites, all over the world, that the initiate be subjected to trials he cannot control beforehand, the positive outcome of which is not at all certain. And yet, the initiate is not cast into this adventure blindly. Most of the time, a long preparation precedes it. He or she is trained and hardened, learns to meditate, and acquires discipline. In this preparatory phase, the apprentice learns to reach the point about which nothing can be learned. There begins the new—the great leap, with all its risks.

The sea of the ancient Celts, the royal chamber in the pyramids of the Egyptians, the wilderness in which Native Americans go on a vision quest and "cry out for a vision"—these are the places where one casts off the old, where one is confronted by a self one didn't know before, and where one is taken up into the mystery.

The one who returns has a tale to tell, a tale recognized by those who have gone before, even though, on the surface, their "leaps" looked very different.

In our time and in our civilization, too, people go through initiations. The external form of the initiation looks different, but the inner change that takes place is the same. In a literal sense, one isn't entrusted rudderless to the wind and the water anymore; different storms and different waves have taken their place. The experience is, however, still equally perilous. When the moment of initiation is there, one still experiences that all depends on that one choice: either give your best and entrust yourself or refuse.

The difference between these times and ancient times is that now the possibility exists for the whole of humanity to venture the leap. It appears that we can only get through our current global crises if we, humanity as a whole, are prepared to leave our old ways of thinking and acting behind. We cannot solve today's world problems in a fragmentary fashion. Structural solutions can only be realized if we are willing to change our attitude toward life. Now the world is the boat in which we are left to the mercy of the elements. The question that faces us, all humankind, is the age-old question of the initiate: Will you give your best and aim for that which goes beyond your own selfish needs, or will you refuse?

This book is the last part of a triptych.* These three books were written independently of each other and stand alone thematically.

---

* Hans Korteweg and Jaap Voigt, *Helen of delen: transformatie van mens en organisatie* (Healing or Dividing) (Amsterdam: Contact, 1986); Hanneke Korteweg-Frankhuisen and Hans Korteweg, *Innerlijke leiding: de kunst om de innerlijke stem te volgen tot in de dagelijkse praktijk* (Inner Guidance) (Katwijk aan Zee: Servire, 1989).

Now, after having finished *The Great Leap,* it becomes clear to us how much they form a coherent entity.

In the first two books, we introduce an integral psychology. The building blocks are a number of seemingly unrelated subjects: the physical body and the tangible bodies, I-formation, image system and karma, the chakra edifice (of age-old Eastern origin), the five character structures (developed by Wilhelm Reich and bioenergetics), and the teachings of the seven rays (known from esoteric writings). We offer an in-depth description of these different systems, and we show how they relate to each other. These are practical books. Their purpose is to help the reader utilize his or her own knowledge and our teachings in daily life.

If we do our work from an attitude of wholeness, that is, if we succeed in uniting the inner and outer worlds, our personality will become the reception station of the higher frequencies of the soul. We will learn to surrender ourselves in receptivity. It will become clear that the work we do benefits others. Then the connection between *I* and self turns out to be a simultaneous connection between *I* and surroundings. The *I,* which previously was a stumbling block, becomes a bridge leading to a new existence. It becomes the gate that leads to initiation. This brings us to the central theme of this, the third book.

One could say that *Healing or Dividing* and *Inner Guidance* provide the building materials for the springboard. In this book, we tell what could happen after building that board: the Great Leap, sometimes called *initiation.*

It is obvious that whoever leaps has to leave the springboard, however solidly it might be constructed. Whoever wants to keep admiring the springboard never leaps. This book is about the adventure of that leap.

From Tent to Temple

We chose as the thematic basis of this book a myth, one of the most poignant in world literature: the myth of Oedipus. We closely follow the Oedipus story, which does not at all mean that we offer every possible interpretation of this beautiful myth. That would be impossible: a myth, like life, always goes beyond any interpretation. We bring forth a number of themes and deal with them in depth. In doing so, we try to illustrate the questions of a person who is facing the Great Leap.

Myths often speak about the path of initiation and the resistance encountered on this path. They serve as indicators that life is a journey on which all forms are like tents. We stay in them temporarily; they never offer lasting shelter. As humans, our biggest problem is that we continuously try to turn our "tents" into "houses," and then proceed to defend these houses with all our might against unwanted influences. We are imprisoned in a world of forms and become lifeless.

For a while, this happens to Oedipus too. But then lightning strikes his prison. He leaves the familiar behind and takes to the road. His house becomes a tent again.

We chose a Greek myth because of its cultural proximity to us and because it isn't contaminated, like biblical myths, with values the churches have attributed to it.

Most churches and religious movements do little else but construct "houses." They construct power structures, amass possessions, and try to maintain themselves through time. They pretend to be keepers of the truth, while their actions are in direct contradiction with the teachings of their great icons.

After almost two thousand years of religious fanaticism, many have started to equate the Bible with the structure builders that have usurped that book. Because of that, the holy books brought together in the Bible are often regarded as outdated, moralizing law books. That is a pity, because in actuality, many biblical stories do not tell us how things have to be, but how we can become free and alive.

We, the authors, think of the Bible as one of the most important books of wisdom, just like the Corpus Hermeticum, the Bhagavad Gita, the I Ching, and the Tao Te Ching. That is why we refer regularly to texts and stories from the Old and the New Testaments and offer our views on them.

In addition to these books of wisdom, we liberally cite well-known and lesser-known authors (see the bibliography). In addition to those, our argument is interspersed with portraits of people, in the form of interviews, diary entries, memories, and dreams.

We hope that these illustrations will make clear that whatever we have to say concerns not only ourselves, and that our message is not restricted to our time and our culture. We are part of a larger whole, an "unstructured order" that has always manifested itself next to and through the "structured orders."

Three of us wrote this book together. This was a unique experience. By continuously tuning in to that which unites us, each of us wrote in his or her own style. Sometimes, our different voices can be clearly distinguished, especially by those who know us. Here and there, one might find some abrupt transitions between the different writing styles and points of view. The end result is, in our opinion, a close harmony.

We would like to thank the people who, anonymously, have entrusted part of their life stories or personal experiences to this book. We can name the following people: Ingrid Eggink-Teeuwen, Joke Brunekeef, and Peter Gerrickens. They helped us tremendously in the development of a series of lectures, the preliminary studies for some of the chapters. Bas Klinkhamer and Hans Wopereis dedicated their careful labor to the glossary at the end of the book.

Finally, we would like to thank Rob Stoeckart, who, with constructive yet unrelenting precision, read and commented on the manuscript. His advice was of great value to us.

The reader who has developed an interest in our work and who wants more information can contact us in writing or by phone at the following address:

Institute for Applied Integral Psychology
Achterdijk 3
5328 JL Rossum
Netherlands
Tel. 011-31-418-662-173

Hans Korteweg
Hanneke Korteweg-Frankhuisen
Jaap Voigt

one

Growth and Initiation

Show me the man whose happiness
was anything more than illusion
followed by disillusion.

CHORUS IN SOPHOCLES' *KING OEDIPUS*

All things born into one form or another are subject to the law of rising, shining, and declining. To put it differently, anything time-bound is subject to growth. Through time, all things shine for a moment or two and then fade away. This is true for the short-lived mayfly, people, even stars. There always comes a moment in which the shine loses its luster and the sinking sets in. Love's honeymoon phase is over, wrinkles appear, the days become shorter again, one's memory starts to fail. The great traitor of all that grows, Death, announces his coming.

As long as all goes well in one's life, few problems arise. Problems do exist, but they are not recognized as such. It is only when things are not going so well that the problems surface. You suddenly notice how edgy you feel, whereas in earlier times every-thing seemed to go so smoothly. But then, even a square marble will glide down an incline smoothly if the angle is steep enough. You begin to realize how dependent you are on external factors. You begin to see yourself and your surroundings in a different light. You start questioning yourself.

When shining passes into declining, people often fall into a crisis.* Crisis can lead to a revision of existence, which, in the end, can result in a fundamental change of one's attitude toward life. This change is what we call *initiation*. It is altogether possible that the only outcome of a crisis is resignation, an acquiescence to the inevitable march of time.

The Chinese character for crisis is made up of two parts, "danger" and "opportunity."

Crisis opens the possibility for the new, but in and of itself, it is impartial. The Chinese character for crisis is composed of two signs, one meaning "danger," the other "chance." A crisis is a dangerous chance and a chanceful danger—it is an adventure.

A crisis, therefore, is equally on the side of maintaining the old as it is on the side of leaping into the new. A crisis urges, tears apart, hurts, but it does not choose. Especially in a crisis, one is absolutely free, since all is uncertain. One possibility is indeed closed off, and that seems to be the end, but on a deeper level many possibilities open up, many more than one ever realized. That is precisely why crisis is so frightening, because it forces us to ask, What is good? What is fitting? Who am I really?

---

* See the glossary for definitions of a number of terms used throughout.

Pride and Thankfulness

While reading an abstract description of a crisis like the one above, it seems obvious which side you are on: the side of life, of course! Don't acquiesce! Into the new! In the midst of a crisis, however, you might not be so self-assured. Then it is difficult not to fuel feelings of bitterness and victimization. You are envious of what others have and ashamed of what you have lost. At night, you are haunted by detailed visions of fear. You lose sight of all proportions. You don't want to deal with anyone and you blame everyone for avoiding you. You feel dulled and depressed. You don't get up anymore. Everyone has his own defenses.

A crisis demands the utmost in discipline. Anyone who goes through such a period successfully looks back at it with a characteristic mixture of pride and thankfulness: pride because one didn't fall into one's own traps too often and thankfulness because it is a miracle that one made it and because success was impossible without help.

Pride and thankfulness are the tenets of Betty van Dam's story *In Search of One's Energy of Life.* In it, she recounts her crisis and how she got through it in great detail:

> Events that profoundly change your life—both you and I have experienced them. One person breaks his neck, another gets a divorce, a third loses a child. All three things happened to me. It was too much, and I started to ask myself, why did all this happen to me? Coincidence?
>
> After my accident (I broke my neck at the age of fifteen) I tried to lead as "normal" a life as possible. I shut out everything associated with disability. I got married and had two kids, but somewhere deep inside of me I felt a dissatisfaction I could not put my finger on. After all, wasn't I "happy"?

Then came the divorce. Annoying, but, well, it can happen to anybody. I lived as a single mother with my two children. To give my life new meaning, I went back to school. Yet even this life didn't really fulfill me, but I kept it to myself. After all, did I have anything to complain about?

In May 1983 my son died in an accident on his way to school. He was almost twelve. For the third time my life fell apart. Luckily, I still had an eight-year-old daughter. I wanted to be there for her, but for myself, I saw no sense in living anymore. This time I was completely crushed.

Why does one person go through life trouble-free, while so much misfortune befalls the next? Is it just coincidence? I could not believe that these kinds of things "just happen." That did not seem fair.

After the death of my son, I started searching for the meaning of life. I read stacks of books, about reincarnation, consciousness-raising, inner growth, meditation, and so on. Through these readings, I reached the conclusion that coincidence does not exist. All one encounters in life has meaning, as long as one is willing to learn from one's experiences. Everything is a part of a larger whole—a whole based on love and aimed at growth.

It takes time to learn from your own life and your own misfortunes. It can take quite a while before you see the light. I myself am a prime example. When I became disabled, I pretended nothing was wrong with me. When I divorced, I acted as if I could finally begin to spread my wings. But when my eldest died, only then did I begin to probe for the Why of earthly existence. Through the death of my son, I started to live again.

In 1987 I enrolled in a study program in healing people. The focus of this program was the complete human being: mind, body, and soul. There I learned a lot about myself. I learned that you create your own life, that you are responsible for your life, and that it is senseless to hold others responsible.

I used to think that my disability was the reason for the dissatisfaction I had felt for years. Now I know I would have felt that way even if I had not been in a wheelchair. I probably would have blamed my mother, or my father, or the church—anything. This knowledge gives you a different view of your disability. Nobody can give you inner peace; you have to find it yourself.

During the course of my studies, I discovered my deepest wish: helping fellow disabled people find harmony again within themselves and guiding them in their search for their own energy of life.

A Conservative Thing

The transition from shining to declining is immediately and most strongly evident on the physical level. But on the emotional and mental level, too, almost everyone is "over the hill" at a certain age. Only a few people grow emotionally after the age of forty, and many people will have reached the end of their mental career at retirement.

When life's shining phase nears its end, one is confronted with the typical stubbornness of the personality. The human personality, the *I,* is a conservative thing. It demands that all be today as it was yesterday, only a little better. The personality panics if growth is threatened, if no continuity is evident.

When the moment of declining has come, the personality will try to deny it with all his might. He will cover up the fact that he can't keep up: he will color his hair; he will see himself in the mirror as more youthful than ever. He will try to pull others into this game of self-deception also, often resulting in harrowing scenes.

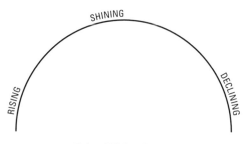

Rising, Shining, Declining

Thus, the personality will use false growth to try to keep his lifeline from descending. Sometimes, people around him don't even notice.

This happens on a small scale to individuals, on a large scale to corporations and countries, and on an even larger scale globally. It happens when people don't want to recognize the discontinuity, when people refuse to make the transition from outer quantitative growth to inner qualitative growth.

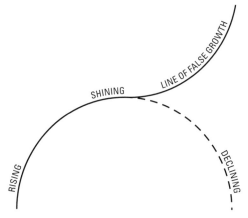

Rising, Shining, Declining—Line of False Growth

This artificially maintained growth cannot be sustained indefinitely. A collapse will always follow, a collapse much more drastic than a gradual transition into declining. Because one has kept up appearances, one falls from an even greater height. It is difficult to find a way out of the resulting ruins.

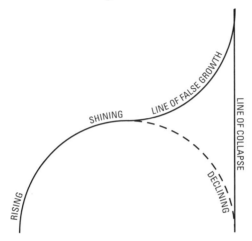

Rising, Shining, Declining—Line of False Growth and Line of Collapse

If one allows oneself to be determined by the automatisms of one's personality, nothing will change. Precisely because one refuses to face death, life is lost. When death finally comes, it devours. In the famous words of the German mystic Jacob Böhme, "He who doesn't die before he dies, is undone by dying."

One is either a child of eternity or a child of time. One becomes a child of time by pretending that only historical time is of importance. Initially, it is possible to be very successful, but eventually all is lost anyway, since time, as we know, devours its children. If, on the other hand, one finds the new that is contained within what was once believed to be impossible, one becomes a child of eternity. At that very moment, one is reborn.

The Tail Eater

In old alchemists' treatises, time is often represented as Ouroboros, the tail eater, the serpent that bites its own tail. Sometimes, the world is depicted inside the boundary made by the snake. It expresses the idea that time surrounds all like a vicious circle. The snake feeds on itself. In continuous repetition, the same occurs again and again, and in this cycle we are born, experience a thing or two, and die.

One can imagine the circle becoming smaller and smaller, because the snake continuously eats a little more of itself. It is inherent in a vicious circle that it seemingly gets smaller all the time, increasing the tension inside. The circle constricts until the

The Ouroboros, the Tail Eater

person living inside feels as though he can't breathe anymore. The feeling of dissatisfaction increases. What at first were vague thoughts and half-dreamed desires become undeniable signs. Things have to change! There is less and less room to move, and satisfaction becomes impossible. This is crisis from the perspective of time.

Anyone not overcome by the vicious circle is able to see that this is a possibility for birth. The crisis is like contractions that push one outward, if one yields. If one does not, one will suffocate. Seen in this light, time is not only a constrictor, it is also a passageway through which one learns and develops until one reaches the point at which one is ready for the new. Then time casts out the child—humankind—spontaneously. This is painful, yet it is grace, because it offers the possibility for new life. In the language of the Mysteries, this is rebirth.

All unwished-for things that happen to us offer the possibility for new life. Everything. There is no meaningless fate. It is meaningless only if we don't dare to take the leap.

This is the principle of grace in disguise.

Grace in Disguise

In his book *Eleusis: The Most Sacred Mysteries of Greece,* Karl Kerényi gives an impressive account of grace in disguise. Kerényi describes how Demeter, the Mother Goddess, comes into the house of King Celeus in the disguise of an old woman, a nurse. She is given the task of caring for the infant Demophon. The goddess puts

> the little boy into the fire each night like a log. She does this
> secretly. His parents don't know this. They are surprised that
> their son is growing into a divine being. The queen cannot
> suppress her curiosity. She secretly watches the strange
> behavior of the goddess and cries out in fear, "Demophon,

my son, the stranger is holding you in this blazing fire!
I lament and bewail you!" Demeter's mood is totally
disturbed. She takes the child from the hearth, puts it on
the floor, and—as his sisters come running to take care of
their little brother—she reveals herself to the queen. In her
warning, she addresses not only the queen, but humankind
as a whole: "Thou art ignorant and thoughtless, O mortals,
thou dost not know whether good or evil befalls thee!" . . .
Demeter would have made the queen's son immortal with
her peculiar treatment. Now he will remain mortal like
all humans.

This is grace in disguise in its highest form. It seems the Great
Mother, in the disguise of a humble maidservant, wants to kill the
royal scion, but in reality she is preparing the child for eternal life.
By interfering, the small (mortal) mother seems loving, but she
doesn't know what is best for her child. She doesn't see *the* child,
only *her* child.

This Greek myth is not a story about a distant past. It is a story
about the present. It tells in metaphorical language what is important. The stranger holds the child—that is, the possibility for new
life in each and every one of us—in the blazing fire! How often do
we have to be put in the fire by the Great Mother before we learn
to allow her to do what is best for us? Precisely because we constantly interfere, motivated by our shortsighted needs, we turn
purification into agony.

The Choice

We are ignorant and thoughtless if we totally identify with
history. As Alice Bailey put it so aptly in her book *Initiation,
Human and Solar,* we wander through the Hall of Ignorance "in
which form reigns and the material side of things dominates."

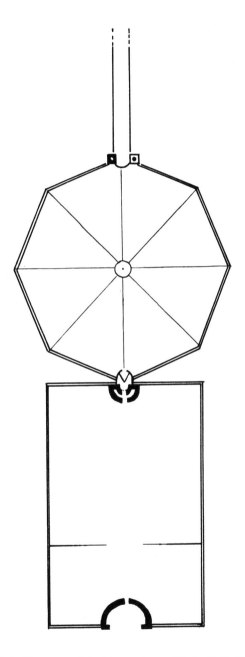

Hall of Ignorance, Hall of Instruction, and Path of Initiation

When the dream of eternal growth is disturbed, a porthole to a different reality might open. Then humans, in Alice Bailey's terms, enter into the Hall of Instruction, where we are placed between the time-bound demands of our personality and the inspiration of our spiritual essence, between the small mother and the Great Mother. We perceive both. Thus, we gain knowledge and experience.

In this phase of our development, sometimes called the *trial path,* we become aware of our good and our nasty habits. We make up the balance sheet. We are curious; we observe, read, and experiment. We learn a lot. A definitive choice, however, is not yet made.

This is still the period of growth. It only ends when the choice is made—a surrender to the Greater that cannot be surveyed and controlled. The choice is always a sacrifice of that which, until that moment, could call itself *I.*

All that is experiencing growth does not know the sacrifice of surrender. Surrender marks the end of growth, and here the Path of Initiation begins.

Growth and initiation are linked together, and yet they are mutually exclusive. Growth is the fulfillment of possibilities given in a certain phase of life. Initiation is the risky venture; it is the leap you take when you leave old possibilities behind. Growth is the conservative way in which life develops; initiation is the revolutionary way. Growth is to initiation what a scale is to music.

A person who dares to leap becomes an instrument played by the great breath of life. The peculiarities and restrictions of the personality are transformed into possibilities through which the silent voice of life can assume its own peculiar sound. Like the instrument it is, the personality, reverberating with, attuned to, and in tune with the great breath, begins to perform life's melody in words and in deed.

Responding thus to the inspiration it receives, the personality meets others who are improvising on the same theme. It discovers that it is playing with others in a trio, a quartet, or a larger ensemble. This is the group of people to which the personality belongs, not by birth but through the willing ear.

I cannot warn you.
An initiation is never the same twice.
Every human being portrays his own experience.

Margaret Mahy, *The Initiation*

Who Does It?

The word *initiation* comes from the Latin root *in ire.* It means "to go in," and "to begin" is derived from it. We can deduce from this that initiation does not happen from external impulses and that it is not executed by others. Somebody passing through an initiation takes a step he has never taken before. He enters virgin territory and is hooked up to an energy characteristic of this new territory. This can be an enormous shock, literally!

Even the resistance encountered by the initiate does not originate from external forces. It is his own resistance—the old life form he passes through on his way to the new, but which he does not recognize as his own yet.

In her beautiful children's book *The Initiation,* Margaret Mahy states, "Every human being portrays his own experience." This is always the case, but ultimately so in an initiation. The initiate's surroundings are an expression of his resistance *and* of his longing to proceed.

First and foremost, initiation is an internal event that only later expresses itself in the world of forms. The fact is that no person initiates another person. However, the deep desire for progress can take shape through another person who appears in one's life as a source of light. This is the basis of "teachership" and "helpership." But even if this person guides you across, he can only do so on the strength of your own willingness. The master who seeks true progress works in the silence of the heart. This is an impersonal process that offers no satisfaction to the subjective personality. When the door to the greater is opened from the inside, the greater absorbs the small—the personality. Is it still me, then? And, as my personality becomes more and more an instrument, will I know in the next instance precisely what kind of life passed through me?

Mahy describes this process in a very subtle way: "At the same time, she felt a light shock in her head like some soft, yet urgent clapping of hands behind her eyes. Then it was as if a wind came in that pushed the silk curtains of her thoughts and feelings aside, passed through them, and allowed them to fall back again."

The Vow and the Ritual

The principle of the initiation is often confused with that of the vow. In actuality, initiation is the transition into a new realm of being. A vow—or its more frequently used modern equivalent, a commitment—is the *wish* to transcend into a new realm of being.

Nuptials can be a vow if a union is at the heart of it. The marriage ceremony, however, is not an initiation. It can be meaningful to make a vow in public, as the creative power of the word increases if it is pronounced in a circle of loved ones. Giving witness to one's deepest desires amid friends and kindred souls breaks the resistance that, until then, hindered the realization of that desire. The effects far exceed any expectation.

Precisely because the spoken word is so generally abused nowadays, we can learn anew the creative power of words. The spoken word is a mighty instrument. Words coming from the heart are building blocks; they not only communicate the message, they make it come true.

Something similar holds true for the ritual, which is also a powerful creative means. There appears to be a close relation between initiation and ritual. We do speak, after all, of an initiation ritual.

And yet, form and being are confused here too. Within the limits of space and time—our spatial temporality—life expresses itself in innumerable forms. We tend to forget the mysterious origins of these forms and instead think that we can make life do what we want by forcing it through forms. Although we know better, we try to control as much as possible because we are time-bound and don't want to die. We want to experience life only within our own values, and especially with no risks. As a consequence, empty forms pile up around us.

Almost all rituals—however deep their symbolic meaning might be—are these kinds of empty shells. They are neurotic attempts to have it both ways, to experience life and, at the same time, to turn it into a consumer good. The knocking at the door during initiation ceremonies, the lying in coffins, and the uttering of passwords are mere children's games for grown-ups who want to taste but don't dare to eat.

Fortunately, there are exceptions. A ritual can also be an invitation to allow an experience to descend into. In this case, the ritual is a form in which one offers oneself to the mystery, and as in the case of the Native American rain dance, one asks the Great Spirit to appear in the world in a particular shape, such as rain. A ritual like this is performed in surrender. The whole wish is expressed, but at the same time, it is clear that "thy will be done."

Many peoples living in harmony with nature know rituals in which the initiate is subjected to the forces of nature (the sea, the mountains, or the desert) to undergo a test. In the introduction, we described an initiation ritual of the ancient Druids. Contrary to neurotic rituals, based as they are on risk avoidance, the nature rituals are not devoid of danger. But even these risky nature rituals do not necessarily result in initiation. The breakthrough depends on how the initiate responds to his situation. It is not important that he keep his vessel intact during a storm. Rather, it is essential for him to connect to a force much greater than any storm, and then to entrust the vessel of his personality to this force, whatever the outcome might be.

Phases

One may wonder whether there are different levels of initiation. Is there an order of initiations?

The great transition, the fundamental step, is from I-directedness to the path of initiation. The path itself consists of many phases, or steps.

Various Western spiritual schools have different views on the details of this path, but especially concerning the first steps, general agreement prevails on the basic tenets. Many schools agree that the first initiation—the transition from the trial path to the path of initiation—is characterized by a crisis of form. In this phase, one learns to subject the physical body and one's actions in the physical world to the higher principle, the soul. Consequently, the key words in this phase are *discipline, attunement,* and *detachment.* The aim is to act in the best of one's knowledge. The personality is no longer in charge, rather it subjects itself. This phase is sometimes called *birth.*

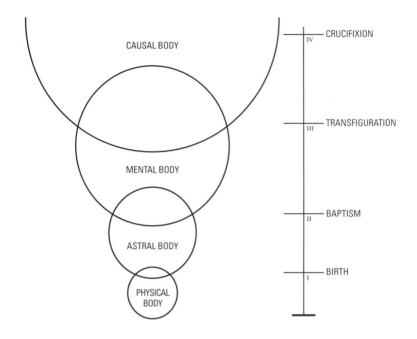

Depiction of the four bodies and immediately to the right of it
the ladder of the first four initiations, from bottom to top:
I: Birth (corresponding to physical body)
II: Baptism (corresponding to astral body)
III: Transfiguration (corresponding to mental body)
IV: Crucifixion (corresponding to causal body)

The second phase is characterized by an emotional crisis. Here, the initiate learns to control his emotional body, which is very different from suppressing it, and he notices how it frees itself from his will and knowledge. If he finally succeeds in cleansing his emotions, in controlling them, and in uniting them with the central source of love, the astral body—the union of emotions and feelings—is not a realm of pseudo-experience anymore. The astral body functions as a mirror that reflects the soul on the plane of physical experience, without distorting or appropriating anything. He who can dwell in the astral sphere without repressing or suppressing anything *and* without being carried away by emotional patterns has gone through the second phase. This phase is sometimes called *baptism.*

The third phase, the *transfiguration,* is a high point in the series of leaps. In it, one learns that the goal of the intellect, too, is not the freedom to do what it likes, but rather to think what one knows and to know what one thinks. In this phase, one experiences that thoughts can create new realities. This is the phase in which one learns to contribute actively to creation as a whole by becoming a creator himself. By truly giving up all dependencies, one professes the existence of the soul. At this point, the personality in its three articulations is a single harmonious and serving instrument.

The fourth initiation is sometimes called the *crucifixion.* Even the high quality called soul is not entitled to an independent existence. The soul is again turned into potential that can assume all forms. As the alchemists say, at this point the retort is broken. The philosopher's stone has formed. There is no self-will anymore. Every expression is healing. This is the state sometimes referred to as enlightenment.

After the first great leap, leading from the deepest dark into the light, continuing along the path becomes more and more a matter of course. Leap after leap, one learns that there is no single ultimate goal. While leaping, the personality learns that life means service and the passing on of knowledge. This is perhaps the most important lesson of the first three initiations.

This continues until, in the end, there is nothing that leaps anymore and nowhere to leap. Then there is no more service and no more passing on. Unity reigns.

*It is certain that no one is an initiate but when he is
absolutely not conscious of that fact and when, on the
contrary, he feels far removed from any kind of initiation.*

J. W. Kaiser, *Geboorteweeën van de nieuwe mens*
(Birthing Pangs of the New Man)

Parables

A few relativizing words are in order. One should not take these initiation phases too literally. They do not capture the truth. The system described here is a mere summary, in logical language, of experiences that transcend the logical. It is a description of an ascending ladder leading from duality to unity. Some claim that this ladder has nine steps, others say seven, still others think there is only one. Many add that, once you are at the top, it does not seem to be a ladder at all, and there is no bottom and top anymore.

Of course, such a system of phases lends itself greatly to dogmatic squabbles and to boasts ("I'm already at the third level; where are you?"). Seen this way, the steps are little more than delusory trinkets for the one who searches. That is not the purpose. They are a symbolic representation, and while they might offer recognition, they do not offer direction.

More important than the ladder and its rungs is the step into the unknown. One does not take that step because a rung is there; instead, a rung forms if one truly takes a step. There are as many rungs as there are real steps that one takes.

The language of cause and effect lacks the ability to describe such a true step, such a leap. To begin with, a different language is required, like the language of parable and allegory. In the words of Jesus of Nazareth in the Gospel according to Matthew, "Therefore,

I speak to you in parables, because seeing, you do not see, and hearing, you do not hear or understand."

Parables are found not only in the Bible, but also in the primal tales that deal with the fundamental questions of life. Many myths and fairy tales describe in detail the path of initiation. In them, the hero must accomplish great feats that are deemed impossible. He leaves the parental home, wanders through the wilderness, encounters along the way what he fears most, solves riddles, is harrowed and tested, looks death in the eye, and, in the end, says, "It is accomplished."

Myths, fairy tales, and even dreams (the myths of individuals) describe nonanalytically the various phases of the path of initiation and the problems the traveler encounters along the road. They describe the mystery without pretending to explain it. It is a living language that, even after thousands of years, has lost none of its direct expressiveness.

One of the most impressive stories in world literature is the myth of Oedipus. It is an excellent illustration of the difference between biological growth and the path of initiation. Part of the myth (the killing of the father and the marriage to the mother) is widely known because of the commentaries of Sigmund Freud. The rest of the myth (and especially the end) is less well known, but certainly no less significant.

In the following chapter, we will summarize the myth of Oedipus as told by Sophocles in the two tragedies *King Oedipus* and *Oedipus at Colonus.* Following that, we will deal more in depth with a number of core themes, and we will relate those to other myths, to fairy tales, to dreams, and to people's questions about life. We will illustrate these themes with situations taken from real life and short interviews. In so doing, we will try to illuminate the fundamental questions that humankind encounters on the path of initiation.

In chapter 10, we will turn again to the various phases of initiation, but this time in great detail. We will do this in regard to a number of concrete themes, namely parents, sexuality, power, and possessions.

The Myth of Oedipus

This is the end of tears; no more lament.
Through all the years immutable stands this event.

CLOSING WORDS OF THE CHORUS IN
SOPHOCLES' *OEDIPUS AT COLONUS*

It will be clear by now that growth and initiation are not limited to any particular time or any particular place. They are inherent in the human condition and, therefore, as old as humanity itself. They refer to the mystery that forms the basis of our existence and that cannot be described in a causal terminology. From time immemorial, these areas of human existence have been interpreted by fairy tales, sagas, and myths.

One can look at a myth in various ways. One can view a myth as the story of a hero who experienced gripping adventures in a particular culture in times long gone by. One can ask whether this adventure contains a core of historical truth and whether it is possible to peel off layers until a factual truth remains: a particular event in a particular historical context. This is the scientific approach of the historian Heinrich Schliemann, for example, who discovered Troy in the last century while for centuries humankind had assumed that this city originated only from the imagination of the poet Homer.

One can also view a myth as an archetypal story that explicates common themes of humanity. The main protagonist is not primarily a particular individual, but humankind in general and, hence, every single individual. Viewed as such, myths, like fairy tales, deal with that which every person knows, experiences, and copes with in his own way. The historical core of the myth is like the thread in an overly saturated solution onto which crystals form. Over the course of time, primeval stories are woven around factual data.

The principle of life, which incarnates as people and other living organisms, is incarnated also in the living word (*mythos* means "word"). Myth formed in this manner always concerns the present, as well.

A fairy tale is "that which is told," a saga is "that which is said," and a myth is "the primal word that creates." A myth is more crystallized and concrete than a fairy tale or a saga. Myths lay bare a primal pattern, mercilessly and inevitably, without frills, without hope of escape, and often without an answer.

Every individual has to find his personal answer to the myth in historical time and space.

The Story of Oedipus

Oedipus is the son of the Theban royal couple Laius and Jocasta. The Oracle at Delphi has foretold that Oedipus will one day murder his father. Therefore, his parents have a shepherd abandon the newborn, piercing his feet with an iron pin so that he cannot crawl away.

The shepherd does not have the heart to commit the child to a certain death. He entrusts him instead to another shepherd, a Corinthian, who, in turn, gives the baby to the king and queen of Corinth.

King Polybus of Corinth and his consort, Queen Periboea, are childless and immediately take to the foundling. They adopt Oedipus and raise him as if he were their own child. As Oedipus grows up, he believes he is the son of Polybus and Periboea.

But then this certainty is shaken. During a drinking bout, one of the guests jeeringly remarks that Oedipus does not at all resemble his parents and that he couldn't be the real son of Polybus. Oedipus asks his foster parents if the accusation is true. They give an evasive answer. Secretly, Oedipus leaves the palace to ask the Oracle at Delphi. The oracle does not answer his question. Instead it predicts a terrible fate for him: "You shall kill your father and marry your mother!"

The Encounter on the Narrow Path

Oedipus is convinced that the prophecy pertains to Polybus and Periboea. As he loves them both, he decides not to return to Corinth. He goes into voluntary exile and leaves Delphi greatly confused. On a narrow forest road outside the city, he meets a man in a carriage. Rudely, the man orders him out of the way. After a heated exchange of words, in which both parties vehemently insist on their right of way, Oedipus flies into a rage and kills the man, his true father, Laius. The first part of the prophecy is fulfilled.

Laius had been on his way to the oracle to ask it how Thebes could be delivered from the Sphinx. The Sphinx—a monster with the head of a woman, the body of a lion, the tail of a serpent, and the wings of an eagle—demands of anyone who wants to pass her the answer to a riddle: "What creature goes on four feet in the morning, on two feet in the afternoon, and on three feet in the evening?" The Sphinx strangles and devours anyone who can't solve this riddle.

The Sphinx

After the fateful encounter with King Laius, Oedipus continues on his path. He heads in the direction of Thebes and, in due course, crosses paths with the Sphinx. She poses the riddle, and he answers, "Man, because he crawls on all fours when he is a child, walks on two legs when he is grown up, and walks with a cane when he is old." By solving the riddle, Oedipus has overcome the Sphinx, who throws herself off the rocks into an abyss. The grateful Thebans reward Oedipus by proclaiming him king in place of Laius, who was murdered by an unknown traveler. He weds Jocasta, not knowing that, by doing so, the second part of the prophecy is fulfilled.

Oedipus and the Sphinx

For fifteen years, Oedipus lives happily with Jocasta. She bears him two sons, Eteocles and Polyneces, and two daughters, Antigone and Ismene. Then fate strikes again. Thebes falls prey to pestilence and famine. In utter despair, a messenger is sent to the Oracle at Delphi to ask what should be done to end the scourge. The messenger returns with the answer: "The banishment of Laius's killer, the payment of blood for blood."

The Revelation

Oedipus promises to find and to punish the murderer, and he orders the blind prophet Teiresias to the court to aid him in this. Teiresias is "the prophet in whom, of all men, lives the incarnate truth." Physically he is blind, but his spiritual eye is crystal clear. Oedipus, on the other hand, can see with his physical eyes but is spiritually blind.

Much against his will, Teiresias tears away the web of illusion in which Oedipus is caught. He reveals the true facts to Oedipus: "I say that the killer you are seeking is yourself." Oedipus refuses to believe him. He is infuriated and calls Teiresias a "peddler of fraudulent tricks, with eyes wide open for profit, but blind in prophecy." Teiresias declares that he doesn't serve Oedipus but rather the Godhead, and he continues:

> You are pleased to mock my blindness. Have you eyes, and do not see your own damnation? Eyes, and cannot see what company you keep? Whose son are you? I tell you, you have sinned—and do not know it—against your own on earth and in the grave.

He closes with these words:

> The killer of Laius—that man is *here;* . . . He that came seeing, blind shall he go; rich now, then beggar; stick-in-hand groping his way to a land of exile; brother, as it shall

be known, and father at once, to the children he cherishes; son, and husband, to the woman who bore him; father-killer, and father-supplanter. Go in, and think on this. When you can prove me wrong, then call me blind.

Still, Oedipus does not cast off his blindness, although sign upon sign reveals that Teiresias is telling the truth. Finally, it cannot be denied anymore, and the terrible truth dawns on Oedipus. He cries out in despair:

Alas! All out! All known, no more concealment! O light! May I never look on you again, revealed as I am, sinful in my begetting, sinful in marriage, sinful in shedding of blood!

At this point, too, the chorus speaks the unforgettable words:

Show me the man whose happiness was anything more than illusion followed by disillusion. Here is the instance, here is Oedipus, here is the reason why I will call no mortal creature happy.

Oedipus tears through the palace searching for Jocasta, crying, "Where is that wife, no wife of mine—that soil where I was sown, and whence I reaped my harvest?" He breaks open the doors to Jocasta's chamber and finds her dead. She has hung herself. With heart-wrenching groans, he unties the rope and lays her on the ground. But the disaster does not end there. The king snatches out the golden brooches of her dress. From full arm's length, he thrusts them in his eyes, "eyes that should see no longer his shame, his guilt." Blinded, he cries out:

O dark intolerable inescapable night that has no day! Cloud that no air can take away! O and again that piercing pain, torture in the flesh and in the soul's dark memory!

Exile

Blind, he leaves his country, accompanied by his daughter Antigone, who leads him by the hand. After wandering for years from one country to the next, he finally arrives at a sacred forest dedicated to the Dread Goddesses. Oedipus knows, with a deep inner certainty, that he has arrived at his destination. He prays to the goddesses:

> Apollo, with the evil doom he cast upon me, promised me also this rest in the time to come, that I should find at last at the seat of the Holy One's sanctuary, and an end of my tormented days; . . . this was the sign he gave that these things should be: earthquake or thunder or the lightning fires of heaven. And now I know it is by your certain direction that I have travelled the road to this sacred place.

Oedipus is chastened by the agony and the many years of exile. He even speaks of himself as "a holy man, here to bring the people blessing." He has gained wisdom. He has experienced in person what he knew in mere superficial understanding as a young man when he confronted the Sphinx: human existence is rising, shining, and declining.

> Time, Time, my friend, makes havoc everywhere; he is invincible. Only the gods have ageless and deathless life; all else must perish. The sap of earth dries up, flesh dies, and while faith withers falsehood blooms. . . . Joy turns to sorrow, and turns again to joy.

Departure and Arrival

In the distance, a thunderclap is heard. Oedipus knows this to be the promised sign, and he states:

God is sending his voice across the sky to summon me to death. [A thunderstorm breaks. Thunderclap follows thunderclap.] Now it is time to go. The hand of God directs me. Follow me, my children. It is my turn now to be your pathfinder. . . . This way. . . . Hermes is leading me, and the Queen of the Nether World. This way. . . . This way.

He takes leave from his two daughters (Ismene, the eldest, has arrived in the meantime):

My children, to-day your father leaves you. This is the end of all that was I, and the end of your long task of caring for me. I know how hard it was. Yet it was made lighter by one word—love. I loved you as no one else had ever done. Now you must live on without me.

They weep and cling to each other until suddenly a Voice, a terrifying voice, calls him. All tremble, hair on end. "Oedipus!" it cries, "It is time: you stay too long." Oedipus departs. Only King Theseus, a newfound friend, accompanies him. A messenger narrates the last he saw of Oedipus:

When we had gone a little distance, we turned and looked back. Oedipus was nowhere to be seen; but the King was standing alone holding his hand before his eyes as if he had seen some terrible sight that no one could bear to look upon; and soon we saw him salute heaven and the earth with one short prayer.

In what manner Oedipus passed from this earth, no one can tell. Only Theseus knows. We know he was not destroyed by a thunderbolt from heaven nor tide-wave rising from the sea, for no such thing occurred. Maybe a guiding spirit from the gods took him, or the earth's foundations gently opened and received him with no pain. Certain it is

that he was taken without a pang, without grief or agony—
a passing more wonderful than that of any other man.

And so, the end of Oedipus. The chorus speaks the final words:

This is the end of tears; no more lament. Through all the
years immutable stands this event.

three

The Cradle

Let it all come out. However vile!
However base it be,
I must unlock the secret of my birth.

<small>OEDIPUS IN SOPHOCLES' *KING OEDIPUS*</small>

Many myths and fairy tales start out with the birth of the main character into an inhospitable world. To protect him from the Pharaoh, Moses is put in a rush basket and entrusted to the river; Joseph and Mary, with the infant Jesus, flee Herod's wrath; and the evil stepmother hands Snow White over to the hunter to be killed. The same fate awaits our main character, Oedipus. His father, who fears being murdered by his son, casts him out.

To some degree, the main character—humankind, every individual—is unwanted when he first sees the light of day. From the outset, he doesn't belong. He is a stranger, a danger to the existing order. However much a child is wanted and loved, he is an unknown factor and, as such, a threat to the status quo of the old existence. In mythical language, the new life is a danger to the old king and queen.

It is the experience of many a parent that, in addition to feelings of bliss over the newborn, the unwelcome thought, "What am I to do with this stranger?" raises its head. Even one's own flesh and blood can be a total stranger.

And sooner or later, every child thinks, "Are these people really my parents? I can't believe it!" Many a child plays around with the idea that he comes from a different planet or that he is really a prince or princess. This theme is used abundantly in sentimental stories and children's books.

The inner certainty that one is a "changeling" can be very strong. As grown-ups, too, many people still suspect that there is a family secret and that they don't really belong to the family. They fantasize that their mother had an affair with another man—their real father—or that they were secretly adopted.

Bad and Good Parents

This foundling complex precedes the Oedipus complex. It originates in the period when the child begins to discover that his parents (and with them the world around him) are not perfect. This can occur at a very early stage. When the child's initial experience of unity with his surroundings is broken—because his needs aren't met in full anymore—the child will attribute that break to himself. He is unable to see his parents and, in a larger sense, his surroundings objectively. He still views himself as the center of all that happens. That is why he will experience the shortcomings of his parents as an act aimed at himself. Likewise, many grown-ups, too, blame themselves for the moods of people in their surroundings and suffer because of this. The child will translate the shortcomings of the parents into being unwanted himself.

For the child, this conclusion is hard to bear. He can employ a psychological trick and create an idealized set of parents and idealized surroundings. Father and mother become, as it were, clothed in a new father and mother who truly love the child very much, who love each other very much, and who are nothing but good. New, child-created parents emerge that hide the bad parents from sight.

In the case of Oedipus, Laius and Jocasta are the original bad parents, who do not want the child and cast him out. Polybus and Periboea are the idealized, good, and loving parents. With them, Oedipus forgets Laius's and Jocasta's existence.

What Cannot Be Forgotten

But true forgetting does not exist. Forgetting cannot last if something is being repressed, just as you cannot forget a splinter that is stuck under your skin even though it isn't visible. Under the surface, one has a constant gnawing feeling, and then when one's guard is down a little (as in Oedipus's drinking bout), the forbidden thought suddenly pops up: *These are not my real parents; my real parents are different!*

Many people experience this when they reach adulthood. Suddenly, through contact with everyday reality, their view of the world is not as rosy as it once was, and that which lies behind it, what has been repressed all this time, becomes visible again. The dream of a twenty-four-year-old man about his father illustrates this. He normally described his father as a gentle man who wouldn't hurt a fly:

> I was in my childhood home. I was walking up the stairs. At the top of the stairs stood my father, his face horribly contorted with rage. I'd never seen my father like this before.
>
> I knew I had to get past my father, but I didn't dare to. For quite a while, I stood there, in fear, unable to move. Suddenly, I shot past my father. He bellowed in rage and

came after me. I ran into a bedroom—it was my parents' room—dashed to the window, and pushed it open. I stepped onto the windowsill and looked down. It was very high. My father was coming. I knew for certain that I had to leap. It was the same kind of certainty with which I knew that I had to get past my father. I jumped. While I jumped, I glimpsed a figure down below, ready to catch me. That was the last thing I remembered.

After this dream, the man gradually started to become aware of the darker sides that every human being has, his father included. More important, he began to see how he had made himself emotionally dependent on his father precisely by denying these darker sides. Early in his life, he had shied away from the rejection he assumed and had remained frozen on his way up the stairs. He had enlarged his father's gentleness and ability to relativize—both true character traits of his father. He had created a new, innocent father for himself, a father whom he didn't fear and whom he didn't really respect, either. This was the father he had to pass in order to "grow up." He had to dare the leap into the unknown out of his parents' bedroom. When he jumped, help was on its way. This was a first step on the path of life.

The Germinating Seed

Psychological insight is, like usual, based on a spiritual truth. Of course, it is very sad when children are frustrated in their needs, when they feel alone and misunderstood. Anyone with a love for children will do his best to spare them pain. But the fact remains that in our temporal spatiality the ideal does not exist, and parents, however loving, are always lacking in one way or another.

Ideal parents or ideal circumstances do not exist. It is paradoxical that the ideal is brought about precisely by the nonideal.

It is the situations that clash with our image of what is needed and necessary that activate the nonideal in us. That is how we develop traits that would have remained dormant in an ideal situation. In the eternally ideal situation, a child would not need to develop these traits. He would grow into a baby with the physique of an adult, and that would be the end of it. Phrased differently, the personal karma develops only in the nonideal situation, and only there do one's real destiny and individuality begin.

The karma—or personal life task—that is viewed and accepted as one's own can be transformed or can be solved in an alternative way. Thus it is the nonideal that offers you the perfect opportunity to become who you are. The undesired causes the seed to germinate. In the terminology of this book, optimal growth demands the ideal; the nonideal is a prerequisite for initiation.

Thanks to the undesired that we experience, we grow our awareness that this world of father and mother is a superficial and temporary reality. We can try to become king in the reality of father and mother, or we can direct ourselves toward the vaguely perceived voice calling out behind it. The Oedipus myth deals with that very conflict.

Daughter Sees Father

We will illustrate this last thought with three portraits of a father, written by a woman at three different stages of her life. The portraits are authentic. The first description was written when she was about twenty:

> My father is a dreadful man. He is impossible to talk to, because all he wants is to be in the right. When people disagree with him, he gets very emotional and starts yelling.
>
> It's as if he's constantly on the lookout to prove that I am egotistic. And then, when I forget something once, he is immediately all over me.

Most of the time, he is not interested in me or any of the other kids. But, sometimes, he suddenly grabs me tightly and pushes himself against me. *Brrr!* I hate that with a passion. Then he has one of those impulses that I am his, or he brags about me to others, in my very presence. I loathe that. It has nothing to do with me, only with what I am able to do and he is not.

And there is more. He is often such an eager beaver. When he is, he makes such a big to-do that everybody has to pay attention to him. And that's not funny at all. But the worst is that he never pays any attention to you.

The second portrait was written about ten years later:

I always have to deal with my father in a very particular way. He never shows any interest in me; he doesn't even know what kind of work I do precisely. He only talks about his own work, about the plays and concerts he attended, about his plans for the future.

Whenever he enters a room, he instantly becomes the center of attention. He doesn't even take the time to find out what the other people are doing; no, he immediately demands attention. He is very preoccupied with his appearance. He is always telling us that people think he looks so young. And whenever a woman comes near him, he instantly starts drawing her attention with suggestive remarks. It embarrasses me dreadfully. He is absolutely tactless. I also find it annoying that he always sees the negative side of things. When I show him my house, he immediately notices the spots that weren't painted perfectly, and he says something about those. When he acts like that, it puts such a damper on my enthusiasm that I feel really rotten. But what am I to do? Not tell him the things that are important to me? Restrain myself constantly and keep telling myself, "He doesn't know any better"?

She wrote the third portrait at age forty-three, shortly after his death:

> My father was full of jokes. And he was always busy with the day to come. He was a sympathetic, lively man. Nice to look at. Suspicious too.
>
> He was a very smart business man, who could open doors with his jovial nerve, but at the same time, he was a very sensitive person. He had a weak stomach, he took everything so much to heart. However, he didn't give the impression of weakness. He was a mixture of somebody who enjoyed life and looked the part, and somebody who was constantly focused on what could go wrong, which was contagious and tiring. It's as if he would have wanted to lead a much more adventurous life, emotionally speaking, a life where everything was possible, but he was constantly held back by this other side. He was often noncommittal, but he also didn't resist the little push to take that step into the deep.
>
> He looked much younger than his age, energetic and suntanned. People couldn't believe he had died.
>
> In his last year, he started painting. With great joy, happy as a child, he painted landscapes, cityscapes, copied from postcards, all freely drawn. The last thing he painted was the arched interior of an old Spanish church. It was very beautiful, with the light coming from all directions.

In the three descriptions, the father changes from a smart-alecky, irritable, and self-centered guy to a person with a number of troublesome character traits to a lively man with lovable traits as well as traits that are hard to live with. When reading the first description, one is immediately struck by how convincingly it is written. Before you know it, you are completely on the daughter's side. Is it possible not to be bothered by a father like that? This woman is absolutely right that she can't stand him!

If you were to form an image of her based on her description, an innocent, decent, altruistic person would emerge, someone who wants attention but doesn't know how to ask for it. She seems to be a woman who suffers much under the emotional character of her father and who deserves our sympathy.

In reality, there is more to it. Anyone who paints a portrait of another person is also always expressing himself. In her portrait, the woman seems to wish that her father would change and pay more attention to her, that he would see her as she is, and that he would settle down. But one can hardly detect anything of that wish in the tone of the description. The tone reveals the author of the portrait. She is a woman who allows herself to be guided by her emotions. She is aggressive and accusatory. She isn't wishing, she is judging.

We may assume that the woman did not see herself, at this stage of her life, as being able to change. A pugnacious spirit speaks from her writing, but she doesn't use that spirit to change herself. She is directing all her energy against the things she finds undesirable.

One experiences a situation as undesirable if there is a difference between the way one experiences that situation and one's ideal image of the situation. Everyone imagines a world in which he would be happy. Such an image is one's heart's desire.

Somebody who doesn't repress his heart's desire anymore but still regards himself as the center of the universe is in real trouble. He can no longer deny that he is wishing for something but won't get it. That is terrible and undesirable! Someone who is completely self-centered will look upon other people as the ones who have to create the happiness he desires. For someone like that, experiencing frustration is the same as dying. There seems to be no alternative than for other people to change. And that won't happen.

The woman of the first description is trapped in this frustration. She experiences herself as the one around whom the world turns. She doesn't know how to deal with her own emotions, and she doesn't want to face up to the truth. She seems to be surviving by projecting like mad. Only someone who also hears a second voice in himself and who begins to realize that the one solution is to change himself, acts this compulsively. At that very point, one can hardly bear the undesirable anymore. Even though she is not aware of it, a fierce battle is raging inside the woman in our example. The crisis is not far off.

In the second portrait, the father's annoying habits are still in the foreground, but he has also developed some human traits. The daughter is asking herself how she should deal with him. She wants to know something. She has opened herself up to reason. Apparently, since her first description, she has changed from someone who couldn't stand to be crossed in any way to someone who criticizes her surroundings but also reflects upon herself. She still stresses her father's tendency to be the center of attention, and that is what she clashes with most. What she can't see yet is that the reason for this clash is her own desire to be the center of attention.

In the third portrait, the woman is in touch with her father. She speaks about him with consideration for his true being. He is of this earth, human. It is moving.

These three portraits are not primarily about the father, but about the daughter. They show the development of a woman from a self-centered child to a woman who is able to see the other for what he is, without making demands. The father changes from being undesirable to desirable. This is not because he lives up to her image of the ideal father, but because she has started to know and love him for what he is.

*And his mother said to him, "Son, why have you treated
us so? Behold, your father and I have been looking
for you with sorrow." And he said to them, "How is it
that you sought me? Did you not know that I must be
in my Father's house?" And they did not understand
the saying which he spoke to them.*

THE GOSPEL ACCORDING TO LUKE, 2:48–50

The Path of Detachment

Back to the hero of our myth: Oedipus leaves his idealized
parents and comes to the oracle, the voice of knowledge that speaks
without taking superficial reality into account. He asks whether his
second parents are his real parents, and the answer he gets goes
directly to the cause. He is told his central karma, his central task
in life: to reconcile himself with the subconscious drive to kill his
father and to make his mother his partner.

That is the karma of all people who identify with their personality. It seems everything will be fine if, as a boy, you become like
your father, only even better, and if, as a girl, you become like your
mother, only even better; if, as a boy, you get a wife like your
mother and if, as a girl, you get a husband like your father. Then
everything will be ideal.

That seems to be true, but it is illusion. If you keep referring to
your parents, you remain a dependent child, and as an individual,
you have lost. You win only if you give your own answer to the
questions and patterns your father and mother gave to you. To do
that, it is necessary to liberate yourself from your father and mother
and to direct yourself to the Great Father and the Great Mother.
If you do that, you will always hear, in some form or other: "Son,
why have you treated us so? Behold, your father and I have been
looking for you with sorrow."

Growing up is only possible if, like the man in the dream, you do not stay at the bottom of the stairs looking up at your parents—if you do not let them determine your behavior. But doing the opposite and merely rebelling won't lead to adulthood, either. The black sheep is part of the family too, just like the Goody Two-Shoes. Both are part of the same system. The solution for the young man at the bottom of the stairs was not to kill his father. If he, like Oedipus, had overpowered his father on "the narrow path" and had thrown him down the stairs, he would never have been able to walk on freely. He would have had to stay in his parents' bedroom, and he would have had to assume his father's role.

The path of liberation is a path of detachment. It is a path on which you don't search outside yourself for the reason for the way you are. Nothing is caused by another, not even by those first two certainties: father and mother.

When you are still attributing something in you to them, you can only liberate yourself from them, from your attachment to them, by forgiving them. Liberation will come only by perceiving them as no child can see his parents: not as monsters and not as gods, but as being good *and* bad, as caught up in the dark in their own way and as searching for the light in their own way. Your parents didn't do anything to you; they were battling themselves. For that you can forgive them.

When you don't feel resentment anymore and when there are no more amends to be made, you are free. You have taken the first step through the gate. You look back in thankfulness, and you rightfully honor your parents.

This so-called working through the father and the mother, central in so many modern therapeutic trends, makes sense only if it serves consciousness-raising. You must become aware of your repressed opinions about your parents and the attachments that have resulted. Merely "working through it," however, doesn't solve anything. You can beat a pillow a thousand times while screaming that you hate your mother because she wouldn't let go of you. But if you don't let go of this image of your mother and the accompanying feelings of hate, you are not letting go of her and you will remain a prisoner—not a prisoner of your mother, but of the karmic system you have created.

Leaving those negative creations behind and, at the same time, viewing "the cradle" freely, make it possible to leave the cradle with love. That is the first step on the path of initiation.

Family Karma

Oedipus meets his father on the narrow path, but he doesn't know that it is his father. They battle for the right of way. His father loses, and Oedipus walks on. Almost immediately, he forgets the incident. In the language of psychology, he represses it. What is so remarkable is that this unconscious deed makes him the exponent of the family karma.

Every family is characterized by peculiarities and recurring patterns to which the members of the clan submit themselves. There are families in which, generation after generation, the same severe diseases occur; families who have secrets (Nazi collaboration, illegitimate children, incest, poverty, alcoholism, and so on) that are kept hidden from the outside world by all its members; families whose members die young; families that go through life in shame; distrustful families; gullible families. Every family has its cross to bear and every family has its karma. Likewise, on a broader scale, every collective that screens itself off from a larger whole will have a price to pay.

The family has a code, a net in which the family members flounder. The net is the bond that represents limits and offers security. For a long time, such a net has a positive function, one that promotes growth. At the same time, however, it restricts, intolerant of development beyond the limits of the family interest. It is not easy to become aware of this restriction. It is even less easy to become aware of the sacrifice that every family member has to make to be allowed to be part of the family, the sacrifice of being oneself.

For example, a person may have a cheerful disposition, but his family code demands a serious kind of thoughtfulness. In that case, the cheerfulness will have to be sacrificed on the family altar regardless of the consequences for the person involved and his individual potential. This sacrifice and association with the family code is what we call the family karma.

What follows is a real-life example of a family karma in three generations. Three sons of three consecutive generations are speaking. They are all twenty-two years old. The son in 1925 said:

> My father is a streetcar conductor in Amsterdam, always merry, always boozing it up. He wastes his whole income in bars. There's nothing left for my education. He is not interested in what I'm doing. I study nights and work days. Sooner or later he has to notice that. My mother understands, she just never talks about it. She keeps saying that I am her help and comfort. I really don't understand what business my parents have with each other.

The son in 1965 said:

> My father was a self-made man. He was already a little older when I was born. He has always been an introvert, and he never gave any sign that he liked me. You can't

really blame him, because he was always either working or ill. Now that I am almost graduating, he has passed away, and I find that hard to deal with. My mother doesn't seem to mind. I will have to take care of my mother now.

The son in 1989 said:

My father left my mother when I was a year and a half old, so I don't really know him. I ask myself whether he is really interested in me. I don't think so, because nothing is working out for me, and I don't see him helping much. My mother has nothing good to say about him. Life's very difficult for her. I help her.

Men Who Hate

By murdering his father, Oedipus really becomes part of the karmic web in which his father had been caught before him. Pelops had cursed Laius when Laius, as a guest of King Pelops had seduced and kidnapped Pelops's son Chrysippus. As a consequence, the curse was that Laius could not have a son. If he were to have a son, the son would kill him. Through this curse and by way of Chrysippus, Laius was connected to the family karma of King Pelops. No small karma.

Pelops was the son of Tantalus, who had recklessly wanted to test the gods. He had butchered Pelops, and from his flesh he had prepared a feast for the gods. However, the gods were not to be deceived. They punished him for his atrocity with the torture that now bears his name. For eternity, he was to suffer hunger and thirst standing in a lake, the water of which receded from his lips, and shaded by fruit trees, the branches of which bent back if he tried to pluck the fruits.

The gods brought Pelops back to life, and he continued on his father's path. He did not kill his son, but he did kill his future father-in-law, King Oenomaus of Pisa, to gain the hand of his daughter, Hippodamia. The sons that came from this marriage, Atreus and Thyestes, hated each other and fought each other in the most horrible ways. Atreus even followed the example of his grandfather, Tantalus, when he butchered Thyestes' two sons and offered them to his brother for dinner.

This is a family, therefore, in which the men do not deal with each other in a loving way. They rob, murder, and deceive. Oedipus is connected to this family. He has to find his own answer to this karma, just as we all have to find our own answers to the karmic patterns of the collective to which we belong. The family karma as a whole is not eliminated when one family member finds his own answer.

At the end of his life, Oedipus frees himself from the web of his family karma. His sons, however, audaciously continue the old pattern. Whoever takes the path of initiation and doesn't see himself as *I* in his family's problems anymore does not redeem his whole family, but he does open a path that other family members can follow. That is the contribution of the initiate to the cradle.

In the beginning, Oedipus takes after his father without being at all aware of it. He sees but is blind. Unwittingly, he continues on his path. The spectator sees how fate gradually builds up around Oedipus and how Oedipus himself provides the building materials. He thinks he is free, but he is a puppet of drives, the existence of which he does not even suspect. Only after he has gained the insight that he is a puppet—that in seeing, he is blind—can he become free. But we are not there yet.

FOUR

The Big Riddle

*The Sphinx forced us to put our own riddles away
for the question he proposed.*

CREON IN SOPHOCLES' *KING OEDIPUS*

Sooner or later in every person's life, there comes a moment at which one no longer benefits from all he has learned, all he has built, and—in general—all he has acquired. The Sphinx pops up in one's existence. All certainties fall by the wayside, and one stands face-to-face with the great riddle of life.

These moments often occur when life shows itself from its darkest and most abysmal side—when fate strikes. Illness, death, misfortune, financial ruin, divorce—these are the most dreaded twists and turns of fate. They bring to light the degree to which we are more than our assumed possessions. What remains when the glamour is gone? What is left when we truly realize that nothing is certain? Despite all prognoses, the future is completely unknown. But then, even the past is, upon close scrutiny, merely a collection of arbitrary representations. Our views of what was and our images of what will be change with our moods.

If the past and the future are not certain, what then is real at this moment? What can you still rely on? At what can you direct yourself?

The *I* derives its self-awareness from its opinions of the past and the future. When those are gone, it is confronted by the mystery that poses the question, "Who are you?" And the *I* has no answer but to be what it is.

The unmanageable and unrecognizable aspect inherent in this moment, this one moment free of past and future, is the Sphinx. Whatever you say *now* and whatever you do *now* will determine what will happen. This is the case at every single moment. Even if you say and do nothing, you are determining your future. Everything is a choice, and everything has consequences you can't foresee. You can flee into one of your pasts. You can bolt into hopeful or fearful speculations about the future. You can lose yourself in the daydreams that make up such a large part of your waking existence, but again and again a voice will momentarily awaken you, the voice that asks you in that very moment, "Who are you? What are you doing? What is your answer?" It is the Sphinx, the voice of reality unadorned.

Whoever is confused by or shies away from the riddle that life poses will be strangled and devoured by the Sphinx. Whoever does not find his own answer or—for one reason or another—does not give it, will lose his energy of life. He will turn bloodless and impersonal. If he does not answer the mystery with himself, he will lose himself. He will become just another face in the crowd.

Process Language as Diversionary Tactic

A contemporary way to try to manipulate reality responsibly is with the use of process language. Many people have reached the point at which they know that all they do is the result of what is within them, not of something external. This has engendered a new language—process language—in which inner developments can be described. In process language, we can create the impression that we are surrendering ourselves to the here and now, while, in fact, we remain in control, just as we did before. We accomplish this by distancing ourselves from what lives in us and by employing our reason to report it.

One example is the reaction of a man to the question: "How are you?" Here is his answer:

> I am totally engaged in regaining some independence in my life; I am learning to make my own choices. For a long time, I positioned myself in a relationship of dependency, but now I am learning that I can stand on my own two feet. This entails a lot of practice at being assertive and facing up to my fear of rejection. I am encountering a lot of unhealed wounds, but I am willing to deal with those now. I have surrendered to the knowledge that all my opportunities are inside of me. It is a difficult affair, but I am working at it. I have no choice, really, because it is hitting me from all sides.

People hearing this nod understandingly. Yes, we recognize that, we are all dealing with it. But that is as far as our engagement goes, because his is a story that concerns the abstract mind. It lacks vitality, it is not personal, it leaves you indifferent, and you wouldn't engage the speaker on any of it. It is, a vague story. But, since it was told with the intention of a personal revelation—the generally accepted mode of speech—the next person will continue in the same fashion.

More concretely, the man's situation is as follows: He is a single man taking care of two children. There is a couple living in his neighborhood who often take his children in. The woman, especially, helps him a lot. For quite some time, he has been having an affair with her, but recently he has fallen in love with another woman, and she with him. Their love relationship has pizzazz. This has made him decide to end the relationship with his neighbor, but he finds it very hard to do this in a good way.

This is a completely different story than the one he has told. You can put yourself in this version of his story, you can understand precisely what his problems are, and you can form your own opinions about them. You can do a lot with this. Anyone who tells his story in this way truly opens himself up. He totally surrenders control over himself, his listeners, and his life. Maybe it even turns out that he is still holding on to some representation that he was not aware of. Humans are, after all, afraid of the new and are often blind to the manner in which they mask their fear. Others have a better eye for the blind spot than you do.

The process as such is not interesting. It is only interesting if you recount how you are acting upon your knowledge and what steps you are taking. Then you are able to tell how and what you experience. This is what helps others, because you are truly telling who you are, what you are doing in your life concretely, and what thoughts are guiding you.

We can bring this kind of a dynamic into our existence by asking that most obvious of questions, "You are telling us all this, but what are you actually doing?"

The Bearer of Death

When Oedipus meets the Sphinx, he has just had his first encounter with death, but the experience hasn't touched him. He simply continues his journey, as if nothing had happened. In his mind, he is in the right, and that's the end of it.

As an initiation into adulthood, many cultures demand that a young man kill a living being, an animal; some primitive peoples even demand a human life. The young man has to perform his task not only without blinking an eye or shirking away emotionally but also without getting carried away by feelings of lust. In this manner, death can be experienced as being a part of life. And it allows us to become aware that we are bearers of death, whether we want it or not. We survive because of the death of other living things.

Oedipus is still a stranger to the realization that death is terrible and sacred at the same time. He is a young man, and the only law of life he knows is the law of rising, shining, and declining. His is the law of the jungle or, phrased differently, the law of shining. He has defeated the old man who opposed him.

It is with this law in mind that he answers the Sphinx's riddle. For him, the answer is self-evident: four is a baby crawling and growing up; two is an adult in the prime of his life; three is an old man who, with the aid of a cane, is nearing the end of his life. It is clear from his answer to the Sphinx that Oedipus knows the law of time-bound growth.

One cannot deny it: it is an answer. He doesn't let the question confuse him, and he doesn't flee. It is the conceited, rational answer of a young man who knows what life is, or rather, what he thinks it is. It is striking, however, that the mystery temporarily retreats because of his answer.

That's how it goes. Rational solutions have the power to make the unmanageable manageable for a while. It appears as if the rule of chaos has ended. In the language of the myth, the Sphinx throws herself into the abyss, into the dark depths from whence she came.

We, the spectators, know that the answer to the riddle did not suffice. Superficial knowledge offers no answers. The Sphinx is only temporarily warded off by male bravura. At any time, she can reappear in another form. We, the spectators of the drama, know that once she does, she can't be defeated anymore, not even by reason.

A fifty-one-year-old teacher says:

> All educational institutions—high schools, vocational schools, colleges, universities—seem to focus nowadays on producing smart alecks. Smart alecks are young people who take in bite-size pieces of knowledge and who, with those, have a ready answer to every question—even to all questions of life. This is the end of life.
>
> There isn't anything to say against the answers as such. They are reasonable answers, all scientifically proven. But they don't move us. In the educational institutions of our civilization, the world as a creative opportunity is replaced by a world in which people, ideas, and information are merely handed down, without attributing any value to them.
>
> The most basic struggles of life (the relationship to one's parents, gender relations, dealing with money, giving shape to one's life in a personal way, dealing with the beast within oneself) are not addressed at all. The law dictates that teachers and students together erect an educational production line, where only catch-all products are produced for a society gone haywire.
>
> In career counseling, no one asks anymore what kind of job suits somebody or what field would make somebody happy because his or her heart is in it. No, the first question invariably is, "What will the needs of the job market be five or ten years from now?" That should dictate one's choice; that is "smart."
>
> Teachers and students who want to stay in touch with the big questions of life are dismissed from the factory. For the factory, these dismissions are mere incidents. "Just act normal" or "Blend in," they say, "and nothing is going to happen to you."

Then the Sphinx will stay in the abyss . . . at least temporarily.

The Animal Within

There is another important aspect to the Sphinx that hasn't been addressed yet: Why does the Sphinx look the way she does? She is described as a monster with the head of a woman, the body of a lion, the tail of a serpent, and the wings of an eagle. What kind of an ogress is she?

Without a doubt, there is a direct connection—as several experts on this myth have suggested—to the astrological fixed cross (Taurus, Leo, Scorpio or Aquila or Hydra, and Aquarius or Man) and the four correlating elements (earth, fire, water, and air). It would indicate that the Oedipus myth originates in the Age of Taurus, which lasted from about 4000 to 2000 B.C. We will not, however, investigate this symbolic or historical line, but concentrate instead on its vital meaning.

Hybrid creatures, like the Sphinx, the centaur, or the mermaid, duly inhabit the world of myths, fairy tales, and dreams. They are directly related to the other creatures that heroes of myths and dreams encounter on their paths: animals.

Just as animals symbolize vital forces or instincts to which the personal consciousness (the main protagonist) must relate, hybrid creatures represent a bundling of primal forces, a clot of instincts. When an *I* starts to form, the animals come to the fore and put their force against the budding awareness of insularity. It is at this point that Little Red Riding Hood meets her wolf, Samson his lion, and Adam and Eve their serpent. In this phase of his life, one has to give an answer, *his* answer, to the things he passed in his development, but hasn't yet integrated.

Growing up, becoming somebody, we achieve by rising above our instincts. We learn to control ourselves; we learn to postpone the gratification of our desires. We suppress the animal, and we lock it up in the basement of our existence. Many of our educational principles and laws only serve to suppress "the animal within." The following dream of a thirty-year-old describes this process:

> I have a kitten, a fierce little animal, that jumps up at me and digs its claws into me. For a little while, I play with the kitten, but then I want to do something else. The kitten won't leave me alone. It gets to be quite a nuisance. It is biting and scratching me. I push it away, but it won't stop. It gets worse and worse. Then my father comes. He doesn't say anything, but I know that he thinks that I should kill the kitten. I take a large knife, put the animal down, and start cutting its throat. The kitten is very strong. I can't kill it. I look up to my silent father to see what I should do. My father nods. I have to go on. This repeats itself several times. I cut and I cut, while my father is watching. Finally, the kitten dies. Then it happens: I look at the limp little animal in front of me, its fur beautifully smooth, and suddenly I realize what I've done. I feel an overwhelming sense of regret. I pick up the kitten, wanting to make it alive again. I wake up with a deep feeling of remorse.

Every person has an "animal" that makes things difficult for him and that demands his attention. Moreover, if the animal doesn't get what it wants, it insists more and more, until it turns into a regular little tyrant. For many people, the only solution then is to take the conservative road—the road of the father—and kill the animal. This is not at all as easy as it seems. But when you finally succeed, it turns out the animal's death does not bring any relief. Without the animal, life is empty; it is lifeless.

The animal in this dream dies in the end. The man followed his father's example and did indeed kill his catlike powers, his sensuality, suppleness, and fierceness. Luckily, our animals—our vital forces—do not have to stay dead forever. They can be reanimated, if we first change some things within ourselves.

The man initiated change because he realized what he had done—in his dream and in his life—and started feeling remorse. Remorse is a powerful force that tears one away from old patterns and liberates, opening up the possibility of the new. Almost three years later, the man dreams the following:

> I walk into the room. Suddenly, I see an enormous black panther lying in the corner. I am scared to death and run out the door.

Upon waking up, his first thought is, "Thank God, my kitten is alive again."

Two weeks later, he dreams that he enters the room and sees the black panther again. He shrinks back and runs out of the room. In the next instance, the door is almost pushed out of its frame by an incredible force slamming it from inside. The panther! Gasping for breath, he wakes up, no longer so happy with "his kitten."

The Returning Animal

After having been rejected for a long time, a returning animal will irresistibly find its way back into a life. A man had the following impressive dream just after his divorce. His marriage had been extremely unsatisfying: it lacked sexuality, the "power of the serpent."

> I am by myself in a modern bungalow built into the side of a mountain. Below me is the ocean. It is dusk. I feel at ease, and I am leisurely looking at the mountain slope above the house.

Suddenly, I see an enormous serpent coming down the mountain, toward the house. It must be twenty-five feet long. I know that all the windows and doors are locked. That makes me feel better. But then I see the serpent coming into the house at the end of the hallway.

I grab the kids—there must have been six or seven of them—and I put them in beds that hang from the wall at eye level. I yell at them not to move.

In the meantime, I have lost sight of the serpent. For a while I look for it, then realize that serpents like to sleep at the bottom of beds. Panicked, I get the kids out of bed again.

I search the beds one by one. I know now that the serpent has to be there. At the last bed, I pull back the blanket and the top sheet, and I reach the bottom sheet. I get ready. I lift up the bottom sheet, and I see the giant head of the serpent. I grab him behind the head, and I spray some sort of insecticide into its mouth. I know it won't kill him, just knock him out. After a while, the body of the serpent goes limp, and I drag it outside through the hallways. I throw it out the door and watch the large body sliding down the mountain. The moment it hits the water of the ocean, it pops back to life again.

It is night now, and everywhere on the ocean I see lights. I know that two of the lights are the eyes of the serpent, waiting for me. I wake up with a feeling of great threat.

The serpent has returned, but it is not welcome yet. It has been sedated and thrown out of the house. Just like the kitten, it cannot be killed. It is waiting for the man. There is no escape.

This dream was so real that, for days, the dreamer would sit on chairs with his feet held high, expecting serpents to be anywhere. He didn't even dare to touch bridge railings; they reminded him too much of serpents.

Yet the man realized that the dream contained a message. He gathered all his courage to get in touch with the serpent, not with its symbolic meaning, but with its energy. He went to the snake house at the zoo and sat in front of the pythons for a long time. He forced himself to look at them and to put himself in their place. He noticed that he most feared their treacherousness, their suddenness and unpredictability. Then he remembered that the serpent is the symbol of healing, and suddenly he knew intuitively that the treacherousness could be transformed into a healing force. He didn't know how, but he knew it to be true, and that gave him strength.

In the end, the main protagonists in both examples were willing to absorb the energy of the animal. By so doing, the energy of a deadly threat could be transformed into an energy that was at their disposal. The biggest enemy of humankind is not the animal within, but our own moralistic attitude vis-à-vis our drives. It is we who make a monster, an enemy, out of our vital energy.

It is a fundamental discovery that negative forces, too, can be known without these forces overpowering the personality, and that, if they are acknowledged, they can be a source of help.

In this way, we learn to know the "animal within" as a friend: a dangerous friend that we should treat carefully and respectfully, a wild friend. We learn what primitive peoples have known for thousands of years: that the most dangerous animal can become a totem that aids and protects, if it is approached in the right way.

The Totem

In fairy tales and myths, the hero is often accompanied by a white wolf, a falcon, a horse, or a fox. The hero endures many a hardship, but the moment an animal becomes his friend, the reader knows intuitively that the hero will reach his goal. When animals oppose him, the situation is critical; if they help him, his tribulations are, in principle, over.

The same holds true for the hero who is dreaming at night. If somebody in a difficult period of his life dreams that an animal loves him, serves him, or helps him, one can be fairly sure that things will take a turn for the better. The wise vital forces are helping him, and that is more important in the end than the insight reason can offer.

In many primitive societies, initiates abstain from food for a long time, waiting until they receive a sign from the animal that is their totem. They are connected to that animal and to the forces that animal represents, for the rest of their lives. They invoke it in times of need. The animal warns them of dangers in critical moments or speaks to them in their dreams. The initiates take great care to be worthy of their animal by living in accordance with its specific energy. What we are dealing with here is a brotherhood of human and animal, where it is up to the human not to suppress the animal forces, but to bundle and project them.

Everybody has a totem. Every person has an animal or a mix of animals, a hybrid creature, waiting in the depths below the consciousness for permission to appear and to accompany him. Sometimes a person lets it wait too long. Then it will come uninvited, overwhelmingly mean and cruel. The animal unleashes its dark side: the serpent arrives slithering treacherously, the fox arrives cunningly, or the bear bluntly and brutishly. If one does not act then, the shadowy side of the totem will gradually overpower him. He will become a werewolf, serpent, or fox. This is a waste of energy, because now these vital forces cannot be employed as aids on the road of life. He will be consumed by these forces, and the human and the forces both lose the best they possess.

Riding on the Tiger's Back

Whoever comes to terms with the animal—with his innate drives—learns to "ride on the tiger's back." The tiger, the foremost symbol of untamed vitality, is conquered. It is mastered by fortitude and control, and the two forces are brought together. The tiger has become the vehicle that follows the direction of the mind while maintaining all its energy.

Learning to ride on the tiger's back means learning to know and to control one's emotions. One is no longer swept away by them. The choices one makes are less and less determined by physical needs and astral impulses. The tiger, when transformed from wild animal to vehicle—to totem—corresponds to the three lower, earth-based chakras. Just like the wild animal, the lower three chakras—root, sex, and solar plexus—can determine one's whole life, in which case the "owner" of the chakras is a mere derivative of his fears and desires.

If the "owner" comes to understand his fears and desires as belonging to him and, at the same time, not to him, these forces can be redirected. At that moment, he is no longer a derivative of his primary energies, his sexual desires, and his ego structure. He has become their friend, he is able to express himself in these realms, and he is able to play in them.

Learning to ride on the tiger's back is the greatest challenge for any person not following the path of asceticism. If one goes beyond father and mother and does not allow himself to be held back in time, he will find the animal on his side when passing through the gate. Walking with the person, on his other side, is a second figure: a figure one begins to distinguish more clearly as his guardian angel, his inspiration and guide. The human is walking in between animal and angel. Both are his travel companions.

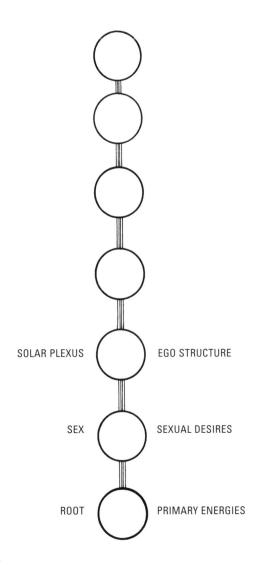

The Lower Three Chakras:
Root, Sex, and Solar Plexus—
Primary Energies, Sexual Desires, and Ego Structure

Through the Gate

The man of the kitten and the panther gradually learned to become familiar with his animals, both in his waking life and in his dream life. After the return of the kitten, a series of dreams followed about all kinds of animals. At the end of this cycle, which lasted for three years, he dreamed the following:

> I am going down a mountain where I had visited a sorcerer. I am not sure whether he was good or bad. I am sitting on the back of a strange creature, a cross between a bear, a wolf, a panther, and a hyena. I am sitting on its back, and I spur it on with my upper legs. It's dangerous, because the animal hasn't been tamed completely. It snarls and growls at me, and sometimes it tries to claw me. I have to be on guard constantly. It is incredibly strong.
>
> I guide the animal down the path. In the valley below lives a tribe of primitive innocent beings. They live off the things nature provides them, and they know no evil. They move about smiling silently. I experience a strong desire to stay with them forever. Separating this paradise from the ordinary world is a large wooden gate.
>
> Then a serpent slithers down from the sorcerer with a message from its master. The serpent coils itself around me and whispers in my ear, "You can choose now. You can rid yourself of the animal. If you choose this, you will have to jump off it very quickly near the gate, run through it, and slam it shut. The animal won't be able to reach you then. If you choose this, the animal will devour the innocent people. The choice is yours. What will you do?" The serpent uncoils and slithers back up the mountain.
>
> I am in front of the gate, torn by contradictory desires. I would like very much to rid myself of the animal, but I love the innocent people. The temptation is great. At last, I spur on the animal and lead it to the gate. I ride through the

> gate. I feel proud and tired and old, but I know for sure:
> this is the right choice, however difficult it is.

In front of the gate, the man had to make a choice: take the road of the father or go into life with the animal. Over time, the animal has grown into its final form. The man can recognize its various aspects now as belonging to him, and he directs it. The animal is still dangerous, and maybe it will be so forever. Now that the animality is directed, the fundamental question arises whether he indeed wants to go into the world on the tiger's back. He still has the choice to live on as "detached consciousness." He opts for the union. That is a big step.

End of Fairy Tale

Oedipus does not take leave of father and mother; he does not learn to rein in his drives. Physically (the parents) and astrally (the animals), he takes the road of least resistance. He answers the mystery rationally, and it seems he is successful. The Sphinx withdraws; Oedipus marries the queen, becomes king, begets sons and daughters, and is loved by his people.

That is how fairy tales end. The myth only now begins.

five

The Sleeping King

Fear? What has man to do with fear?
Chance rules our lives, and the future is all unknown.
Best live as best we may, from day to day.
Nor need this mother-marrying frighten you;
that is nothing; many a man has dreamt as much.
Such things must be forgotten, if life is to be endured.

JOCASTA IN SOPHOCLES' *KING OEDIPUS*

Having ostensibly overcome the Sphinx, Oedipus receives a hero's welcome in Thebes. He marries Jocasta, the wife of King Laius, who was murdered by a stranger on a faraway road. Oedipus and Jocasta love each other, and two sons and two daughters are born. Oedipus is a wise and resourceful monarch, beloved by his people. Fifteen years of prosperity ensue.

Since this episode lacks any dramatic tension, it is tempting not to pay any attention to it. All people concerned are thriving, and unless you are one of them, this scene is completely uninteresting. Yet, this period of happiness is meaningful in a dramatic sense too. As spectator, one senses how great the gap is between the outward glamour and the underlying truth, precisely because everything seems idyllic and innocent from the outside. You realize that the denouement is coming closer and that the longer this time of blissful ignorance lasts, the more catastrophic the outcome will be.

The Sleeper, by Jan Uriot, Print 53 from the *Exodus* Cycle

As spectator, one identifies more with the Oedipus of this period than with the Oedipus of previous years. You recognize this scene. You are that king. Everybody longs for that happiness, for the peace and the comfort. And when you have reached that happy state temporarily, you will also recognize the gnawing feeling that maybe it isn't so good after all, that the peace could suddenly be upset by disaster or misfortune. You become the main protagonist *and* the spectator of the drama. As protagonist, you want the happiness to last an eternity. As spectator, you know that this is impossible and that you will lose it. You realize, after all, as a spectator, that this happiness is not built on knowledge and acceptance of life, but on denial and flight from life. It is the happy state of dormancy from which you can wake up at any moment. It is the Great Sleep.

Forgetting the Great Work

On an archetypal level, numerous examples of the Great Sleep exist. In fairy tales, princes, bewitched by false princesses, fall asleep and no longer recognize their true loves. Sleeping Beauty lies in the midst of an overgrown garden and awaits the kiss that will awaken her. An alluring sleep always comes, in which the great task one was engaged in is forgotten, and from which one is awakened by a beloved.

We are familiar with the moving story of Jesus and his disciples in the Garden of Gethsemane. Jesus asks his disciples to stay awake with him in his last night. They promise to do it, but again and again, they are overcome by sleep.

> And being in agony he prayed more earnestly; and his sweat became like great drops of blood falling down upon the ground. And when he rose from prayer, he came to the disciples and found them sleeping from sorrow, and he said to them, "Why do you sleep? Rise and pray that you may not enter into temptation." (Luke 22:44–46)

Jesus, the guiding principle, is looking at death. He is standing in reality and is sweating blood and tears. That which follows the guiding principle but remains partly blind (psychologically speaking, these are aspects of the personality) can only stay awake for a short time. Then it sinks back into outer appearances, into favorite dreams. Each time it is awakened again by that most inner voice, each time it has to admit shamefully that it has forgotten all it knew, and each time it falls asleep again. This continues until the discipleship ends and the apprentice is not awakened anymore, but has awakened.

A thirty-year-old man dreams the following:

> I am walking to a rickety old shed. I have to clean it out. In the shed, large cocoons are hanging from thin silken threads. They are swaying ever so softly. I have to clean those up.

This man is on the verge of beginning a new life. He has met a woman and fallen in love with her, but as yet he is still completely absorbed in "the bosom of the family." It is he who is swaying softly in a protective and blissful state of dormancy inside a cocoon. He is also the man who wants to cut the threads and clean out the old shed. He is sleeper and waker in one.

A Sleeping Beauty

Anyone entering the path of initiation awakens from the Great Sleep. This does not mean that he will never again fall asleep, will never again lose consciousness, or will never again forget what he was doing, but he does know what it is to be awake.

Anyone who does not exclusively follow the path of rising, shining, and declining can distinguish periods of sleep when looking back on his life. He knows when he was jolted awake, grumbled, rolled over, and snuggled up under the blanket again, and when he woke up. The following autobiographical story of a woman describes this awareness:

> Until I was twenty-five, I didn't know what it meant to be myself, because I didn't want to be different from others. I never wanted to do anything that anybody else would disapprove of. But I was very intelligent, so I did my best to be good in school. I was so good I was almost different than others, but not quite, because better is not different. It was very much appreciated.
>
> I always tried to mold myself into other people's thoughts, but I never really managed to do it because, at the same time, I considered other people's thoughts to be dumb. I understood very well how they didn't add up, that their thoughts were always centered on themselves and that, therefore, they were shortsighted. The people themselves didn't figure that out. That is why I never really had contact with other people, and I was always a little tense. I looked at myself, I heard my own words. I had a strong sense of artificiality. Once in a while, something would spontaneously come forth from me, when I hadn't been thinking. I would try to hold on to these moments, to repeat them, but that didn't work, of course.
>
> I admired people who were witty and genuine, who would spontaneously say what they thought. But I couldn't associate with them, because, after all, I was a bore. To me, what others thought of me was more important than what I thought. I had no real experiences. The only stories I had to tell were reports of factual occurrences.
>
> In short, I lived in a looking-glass world. I was constantly looking for an entry outside of myself, which did not exist. I didn't talk about this with anybody. Not because I didn't want to, but because my own thoughts and feelings didn't represent reality for me. Moreover, it would have meant the end of my existence.

I recall that time as though I'd been infinitely veiled. I know that things happened, but I don't know how I felt about them. I don't know whether I found them nice or horrid. I do know that I had this great fear of forgetting something or making a mistake. Then I would desperately try to find the source of that blank in my mind, so it wouldn't happen again.

At one point, I even got married without any direct contact. I did feel some closeness and some kind of warmth with my husband, once in a while. That was nice. But one could hardly call it real contact, there was no giving and taking. I assumed that he wanted me, and I responded to that. When he started to lose interest in me, I became aggressive more often. We quarreled a lot, but it never crossed my mind to leave him. I had never been alone. It was better to be frustrated together than to be alone.

I was twenty-five when, for the very first time in my life, I went away somewhere on my own for a couple of weeks. I ended up with people who lived in an atmosphere where lightness and relaxation were stressed. There I happened upon a book by Ouspensky: *The Psychology of Man's Possible Evolution.* When I read this, the veil was lifted. I knew that this was the truth. In it I read, "People resemble machines. Unwittingly, they are asleep. They identify with everything they are not and consider everybody else. They can only wake up if they become aware of this. It is necessary for them to remember themselves. Then it becomes possible to develop this further, freely and consciously."

That is when I woke up. The fog in my head was lifted. I was someone I had always been and would always be. I had known that all my life, without realizing it. That was the beginning of freedom.

Row, row, row your boat
Gently down the stream,
Merrily, merrily, merrily, merrily,
Life is but a dream.

NURSERY RHYME

Blissful Oblivion

Few things are as nice and as comfortable as sleep. Isn't it delightful to be able to forget everything and, as it were, to be completely submerged into something that fits you so snugly? To have no self-awareness, oblivious to all your doubts and worries? You have no obligations when you surrender to Morpheus, the god of dreams. It is not surprising, then, that we human beings have tried in every way to prolong this blissful state and are still trying to do so.

We have developed a phenomenal capacity for producing means to eradicate all friction in our existence. We don't even have to notice that we are alive. The pharmaceutical industry and the medical profession help us to avoid feeling any physical pains or frustrations. For psychological problems, we can consume psychopharmaceuticals and, less openly, alcohol and a large variety of drugs to correct our moods. Almost everyone finds these very acceptable to use, if, in some way, they don't "feel good."

Feeling good is the most important thing there is for the sleeping person. He will do anything for it. It determines his choice of friends, the newspaper he reads, and the political party he votes for. He follows leaders who promise him the best feeling, and it is very important for him to be good for others.

One person likes this, another does not. We cannot argue about personal taste. One person may love to be in charge, and another may love to be led. While their preferences can take many different forms, when you look carefully you will see that both people have one thing in common: they both position their point of reference outside of themselves; they both require an external element to keep feeling good. The master is dependent on the servant, the servant on the master. Both are slaves to their dependency.

The sleeper is dependent on his surroundings. He doesn't want to know this, but he doesn't want to change it, either. He will make sure that his surroundings keep administering the soporific he needs. This is how the people in the sleeper's surroundings become the main protagonists in his dreams.

We asked the woman who gave the account of her dormancy what was so satisfying about her unsatisfactory marriage, and why she kept it going for so long. She responded:

> I didn't have to change. I didn't have to expend any real effort. It seemed as if my husband was as mean to me as I was to him. But I knew that I was really the one in charge. And I knew also that he wasn't going to change. I didn't want him to, either, because now I could do whatever I wanted. I didn't have to care about him at all. I could drink as much as I wanted, pick up guys, do whatever I felt like. And that's what I did. Sometimes, I would be mad with jealousy, but I knew that, in the end, he couldn't do without me. And even though I didn't say it, I could do without him. I had a real sense of power. I told myself, "What I am doing now is just playacting. I'm just pretending to have this husband, pretending that this is my work, and pretending that these are my friends. But when I meet someone who really sees me as I am, then everything will be different." That's why I was never really afraid. I was the one in charge. If I really wanted to . . .

[Let me assure you that] there is absolutely no reason for concern. Of course, the global situation demands our constant attention. But that is a matter unrelated to anxieties for our immediate safety. I stress again, there is absolutely no reason for concern. The more we regard the situation with equanimity, the more judiciously we attend to our daily business, the better it will be for ourselves and the more favorable impression it will leave on the outside.

DUTCH PREMIER HENDRIKUS COLIJN IN A RADIO ADDRESS
ON APRIL 11, 1939, ABOUT ONE YEAR BEFORE THE
NAZI ARMIES MARCHED INTO HOLLAND

No Reason for Concern

People sleep as individuals, but they also sleep collectively, and they will try to keep themselves and others asleep collectively. This is often done with messages such as, "There is no reason for concern."

We live in a world in which we are constantly put at ease. We hear soothing piano music when a plane is landing. Large malls have a comforting "acoustical wall." There is no reason to panic. Never ever. Our politicians can be seen on television as humane but also wise statesmen. They explain that, of course, some things will have to change, but things are fine in general. Very fine.

Every day, television, newspapers, advertisements, and a myriad of organizations dish up hundreds of comforting messages for us. The general tenet is: "Don't worry, we are thinking of everything. We are taking care of everything. Close your eyes and sleep." Moreover, for a nominal amount, we can insure ourselves against anything risky, including our lives.

The price we pay for this happiness is keeping our heads in the sand—the price we pay is sleep.

The promise that we can simply proceed along the present course is *the* lullaby of our civilization. Politicians, state officials, and managers of large corporations are the guardians of our collective lullaby: societal continuity. As captains of the ship that keeps sailing on, they make minor adjustments to the course. Of course there are problems, but they are there to be solved. As long as we keep thinking positively, along with our leaders, there isn't really any reason for concern.

And above all, we must realize that we have to be realistic; that in a democratic process compromises will have to be made; that life consists of giving and taking; that history proves that change occurs gradually; that it is absolutely necessary for there to be a period of adjustment to the changing circumstances, and thus not everything should be changed at once; that it is very difficult to determine the extent of the necessary changes, as everybody should be heard; that new impulses are always welcome, but of course, not every initiative can be honored; and that no further comments on this matter will be forthcoming.

We hear thousands of these phrases each day, spoken aloud in a collective sleep—internationally, nationally, in cities, in clubs, in families. Comforting phrases that reassure us that things aren't that bad. Phrases that tell us not to get upset, and if we do, well, we are the ones with a problem. But we can get help for that.

In the following passages, we present three portraits—from life—of people in an organization who each contribute on their own level to the collective sleep, thus becoming three sleep-inducing guardians of continuity. The CEO speaks:

> In this part of my New Year's message, I want to address
> the rumors that have been going around in our company
> for a while now, that we could be facing a major reorgani-
> zation. As you all know, the market situation in our branch

has drastically changed in the last couple of years. It is our challenge to find a response to that. This means that we will have to mobilize all our forces in order to regain our leadership position.

The general tone I want to set here is not one of looking for scapegoats within our organization. Everyone has given their absolute best in the last couple of years, and we can be very proud of the expertise we have built up. I would like to stress here again, as I have previously done in meetings with your representatives, that there will be no forced layoffs. During the transition phase, which we are facing now, our forces will be aimed at guaranteeing continuity for our employees.

We are going to start a number of initiatives that, in the long run, might lead to a number of inevitable structural changes. I am thinking here of initiatives that will result in the reduction of costs, a streamlining of our automation system, a more customer-oriented business practice, and quality control on all levels. We will also appoint a committee to decide which vacancies to fill of those that open up through natural attrition.

Let me assure you that we will have extensive consultations with all parties concerned, before we introduce any measures. On the other hand, the operating results of the last couple of years and the short-term outlook compel us to enter into a phase of reorientation. I am convinced that, if we work together, we will once again become an industry leader. I would like to raise my glass in a toast to this, our goal, and wish you all a very happy New Year.

A consultant (with spiritual training) speaks:

Of course, it is hard to make these kinds of far-reaching decisions. We are, after all, dealing with people and their futures. Therefore, a period of rest is called for in order to further crystallize the presently attained insights into a single clear vision that can be communicated. This simple but very fundamental vision will have to be captured in a few distinct words: spearheading into the future.

It is of great importance to create a sufficiently broad base of support. For this, practicing effective communication and addressing questions in such a way to show that we truly *care* is necessary.

We will be spearheading change with a basis of broad support. We can apply the age-old principles of yin and yang here. To reinforce this, I have brought a copy of an article in the *Harvard Business Review,* "The Integration of Archetypes in the Organization," for you.

Allow me to address the question of how this reorganization will affect you personally, because only when this has become clear can you—each and every one of you in your particular functions—bring a total dedication to the process. It is my recommendation that you as individuals take part in a personal retreat for a couple of days. It will facilitate a confrontation with your own selves, from which you will glean all the data to face up to your surroundings. During these days, you will also be able to study the various spiritual trends (we might even call them "movements"). After all, they do offer many an opportunity that can be applied to the business practice.

The middle manager speaks:

Well, sir, I have been around for thirty years now. I started out in the warehouse before there were even any forklifts. But let me tell you, nothing ever changes here. Once every couple of years, I get a new boss. I've had about twelve so far. Mostly nice people, younger, who want to get higher up. But let's be real. The way I see it, production has to go on, preferably with as few people as possible. Machines have been taking over for the last twenty years, but those decisions are made in a different department. I don't make production decisions. So, what do I do? Well, I try to keep it fun for all the men and women under me. And that gives me enough problems. Always the same ones.

The director's New Year's speech? I have witnessed four major reorganizations. My work doesn't change. At the most, I get a few more people under me, and there'll be a few new forms I'll have to fill out every week. They live in their own world up there, we don't hear much from them. I'll have to stick it out for another ten years. I'll survive. Pensions are good here. You know, all in all, it ain't that bad here.

Adrenaline Addiction

In these three portraits, the speakers are people who, although active in appearance, are engaged in preventing any real change from occurring. For them, activity is like a drug that anesthetizes their awareness of the situation.

To truly wake up, it is necessary to find tranquillity first. But pity the one who tries. If he tries to find peace and calm, he will be besieged by images of all the things he still has to do. The strongest voice, audible above everything and urging the most insistently, is saying, "Where is this leading, what will the results be, and what happens after that?" This is the leader—the voice that wants continuity, a guarantee for the future.

This voice is the sickness of Western civilization. It is because of this voice that we lost contact with the earth. The ego is in a hurry, because around it the world turns. Anyone who begins to seek tranquillity above the urge to produce will notice how lonely this endeavor is. Even more so if he visibly starts to organize his life around tranquillity. Everything around him seems to urge him to keep on running. Society as a whole seems to be based on this, a deeply rooted addiction to adrenaline in the blood. Everybody gives in to this addiction under the disguise of "I have to do it, otherwise . . ." At the very moment someone wants to come to a halt, he is faced with something bigger than his own restlessness. He is faced with the manifest restlessness of the world as a whole. Are you thinking of quitting your job without having another one? Do you want to start taking it easy without any visible material rewards? Everyone will remind you that you are crazy. You are not going to the party because you want to be alone? They say, "You must be sick."

It is the haste of the personality that doesn't realize that the soul has all the time in the world. It is fear of death that keeps us running.

Anyone wanting to rid himself of this has to be very strong. One's sole inner drive has to be a desire to end the collective sleep, to give the earth another chance. And one has to love oneself very, very much.

The New Age

The established order has solid arguments and soothing charms not to wake up. But on the opposite side of the line—the alternative side—people maintain their own fashionable fallacies too. That side also only pretends to be awake, so one doesn't really have to wake up.

One of these modern fallacies is a blind belief in the New Age. It is a rather deceptive packaging of the sleep, because it gives the impression of being spiritual. It pretends to depart from a deep trust that all will take a turn for the better. One hears, "The whole of humanity will, slowly but surely, be persuaded of the existence of a higher dimension, a world of light. That force is stronger than all evil. If only we unite ourselves as brothers and sisters in love, unity will take hold in the world spontaneously. There is nothing to be afraid of."

In essence, these kinds of thoughts are positive, but if we don't go beyond them, nothing will happen. Their sole function, then, is to soothe the fear for a future one secretly dreads. They negate the reality that is becoming more and more threatening. Thus, they serve cowardice.

A few examples of this way of speaking follow:

> "I know that I really am one. I am working on reaching this wholeness, so I can assume my place in the larger unity."

> "It is essential for me to heal myself, then the earth will heal, because I am an integral part of it."

> "There is a personal lesson to be drawn from the fact that that smelly factory was built next to my house. It teaches me to be more receptive."

> "The fact that this is happening to me now is the result of the karma from a previous life."

If you sum them up, these invocations say nothing more than what sleepers have always said, "It is none of my business; let others make things better; I'll take care of myself." Only the finish is new, and to all eyes it is very altruistic: "We are at the threshold of a New Age in which painless unification will be the reward of human kind."

The Pearl

Until now, we made an encircling motion in this chapter, and we described the Great Sleep in a number of ways from the outside. We explained, with some examples, the role sleep plays in personal lives and in society. After all this, however, the question still remains: what precisely is the Great Sleep?

This question is answered in an expressive manner in "The Song of the Pearl," a story that dates from around the beginning of our era. The story begins with a heavenly prince who is sent to Earth by his parents to find a pearl in the darkest of all regions (Egypt). The pearl is in the middle of a sea surrounded by a hissing snake—in other words, in the realm of the Ouroboros. Our young hero begins his journey cloaked in the dress of the earthly humans. He incarnates and takes on an earthly form. He does that

> so I would not look like a stranger, not as someone coming from abroad to rob them of the pearl, and so they would not awaken the serpent. But somehow they did notice that I wasn't their compatriot. They approached me and prepared a drink of their guile for me, and they offered me of their food. I forgot that I was the son of a king and I served their king. I forgot the pearl, for which my parents had sent me. The heaviness of their food made me fall asleep.

What a beautiful metaphor. A stranger, the soul, cloaks himself in an earthly form and falls asleep because of the heaviness of the food. He becomes as the others, an isolated individual, a personality who has no inkling where he came from or what his task is. He has a false sense of self, like the leaf of a tree that thinks it exists in its own right and doesn't know that it is a part of a gigantic tree. *That is the Great Sleep.*

This is not the end of the story of "The Song of the Pearl":

> My parents witnessed all that befell me; they were saddened because of me. . . . A message was sent, ". . . Wake up and rise from your sleep. Hear the words of this letter. Remember that you are the son of a king, be aware of whom you are serving. Think of the pearl, for which you journeyed to Egypt. Remember the royal attire, so that you

> wear it and adorn yourself in it, and so that your name may
> be read in the Book of Heroes, and so that . . . you may
> inherit our empire."

The soul falls asleep. It forgets its origin, but it is not forgotten. The origin does not fall asleep. Continually, memories keep popping up during sleep of how it could be, of the original form, the royal attire with which one can live in time and space, and yet remain free. Dreams, events, other people, books you read—they all remind you of who you truly are, until the message becomes an inner voice that penetrates sleep.

> The letter was like a messenger. . . . It rose up in the form
> of an eagle, the king of all birds, came down to me, and
> became a voice. Because of it, I woke up from my stupor
> and I arose. I took the letter, kissed it, broke the seal, and
> read. The words of the letter were completely the ones that
> were written in my heart. I remembered again that I was
> the son of a king and that my free origin longed for its
> essence. I remembered the pearl again, for which I had
> been sent to Egypt, and I began to cast a spell on the
> hissing serpent by calling out to it the names of my Father
> and Mother.

He who wakes up remembers and knows again that he is free and part of the unity. He realizes that he can find an essence—the pearl—in a world of duality, the world of the hissing serpent, and that he can bring it back to the origin. He can achieve this only if he, time-bound as he is, reminds himself constantly that he is a child of the Great Mother and the Great Father. Only then does the fact that he is bound in time and space lose its grip on him. Only then can the spatial-temporal become again what it is: a field of expression. Now sleep has truly ended.

Thus I grabbed the pearl and turned to go back to my Father. I took off the dirty and unclean dress, left it in their land, and directed my steps. . . . The letter that had awakened me from my sleep went before me, and just as it had awakened me with its voice, it now guided me with its light that went before me, it guided me with its voice, and it pulled me toward itself with its love.

The Food of the Sleeper

The prince in "The Song of the Pearl" wakes upon the arrival of the eagle. He could have chosen to withdraw even further. He could have eaten more of the earthly food, which would have made his sleep even deeper.

Besides a false sense of self, we have a false sense of the world, of others, of everything we don't call *I*. If, in our apperception of the self, we disconnect ourselves from the totality of life, we disconnect the rest of life from ourselves at the same time. The inner connection is broken. The only contact left is through our senses. We perceive other aspects of life as if they were objects, outside of us.

Then we try to establish a relation with these objects: we study them; we judge them beautiful or ugly, interesting or obnoxious; we love them; we need them; we enjoy them; we use them. The more we believe that these relations constitute reality, the deeper our sleep is.

An immediate consequence of the false sense of self is the loneliness and fear that the isolated *I* feels. It needs the other and the others, but at the same time it fears them. It craves connection and association, but it doesn't want to lose itself. To satisfy this craving, the *I* develops a number of possibilities so it can form a relationship with others without being affected by the relation. These possibilities are the "earthly food" of which "The Song of the Pearl" speaks.

There are many kinds of "earthly food." There is something to everyone's liking, but on top of the menu are three "specials of the house": power, sex, and possessions. Each and every isolated personality is deeply devoted to these three things.

The personality anchors itself in power, sex, and possessions. Once it consumes these three, it feels that it truly exists, that it is good that it exists, that it is not alone, and that it won't die. This comforting feeling, however, is only temporary. That is why it has to consume the food frequently, preferably in ever-increasing doses.

He who wakes up develops a different relationship to sex, power, and possessions. The reverse is true too: he who develops a different relationship to this food wakes up.

Some spiritual schools consider these three powers so dangerous that they advise their more serious students to abstain from them completely, to strictly develop a relationship with them based on rejection. They declare that one can only remain pure if one abstains from this "earthly food." That is why, to give one example, one has to take a vow of chastity (sex), poverty (possessions), and obedience (power) to be admitted to a Roman Catholic monastic order.

We don't believe that possessions, power, and sex are self-contained evil forces. They are powerful drives that can possess someone, but they are also potencies that can serve as the raw materials for a process of transformation, an alchemical process. One's consciousness cannot be affected. If one eats this food consciously, "lead" can be turned into "gold." We will deal with this process of transformation in chapter 10.

Again the Sleeping King

Let's test out our knowledge of sleep and of the continuation of the state of sleep against the story of that other royal son, Oedipus.

Oedipus's adventure began when he started asking himself from whom he was truly descended. That question was a wake-up call. He broke away from the position he had attained (power), left his possessions behind, and journeyed to the oracle. There he was told that he would kill his father and marry his mother. Based on his erroneous notion of his birth, and because he identified with the oracle's prophesy, he fled and, consequently, killed his father.

When he continued his journey, he came face-to-face with the Sphinx. In this encounter, he was again thrown back to the question of his identity. "Who are you now?" the Sphinx asked. This represented a second opportunity to wake up. But Oedipus didn't. He gave the best answer he could give as a sleeper, and he described the course of life, of the *I* bound in time.

For this he was rewarded with the highest one can attain in a dormant existence. He became a king, his father's successor, honored by all (the highest power). He became rich in money and possessions, and he was blessed with children. He was rewarded with Jocasta, the beautiful queen, as his wife.

This last circumstance requires explanation. If this is the highest a sleeping person can attain, why is he rewarded with his mother as his sexual partner?

Of the triad of power, possessions, and sex, the most dangerous for the *I* is sexuality. When you exercise power, you can remain an outsider; possessions you *have;* but in a sexual relation very quickly, you yourself are directly involved. You could regard the other as a mere sex object to satisfy your lust, but such a relationship would quickly turn empty and joyless. You cannot merely rub yourself against the other; you will also have to surrender yourself to truly enjoy sexuality. The *I* regards that as the greatest danger of all.

In surrendering, you have no boundaries anymore. You allow the other complete access to you. You empty yourself completely in the other, with no reservation, with no self-apperception. You are eye to eye, heart to heart, with the other, the unknown. The *I* longs for this fervently, but fears it to the same degree. All paranoia about life surfaces. Shame and insecurity pop up—everything the *I* does not want. And yet . . .

How glorious and how secure it would be if you could totally give yourself, as a man, to a woman who knows you inside and out, the woman from whom you came: your mother. And vice versa: how glorious and how secure it would be if you could totally give yourself, as a woman, to a man who knows you inside and out, and who is always there for you: your father. You could forever remain the little boy or the little girl.

It would be especially delightful if you didn't know that he or she is your father or mother. You could give yourself over to innocent enjoyment, you could be taken by the hand, and you wouldn't have to take any risk, because he or she would bear all responsibility. You wouldn't have to venture into the unknown.

Lots of men and women wish for a partner to whom they can surrender themselves, whom they could enjoy, but who isn't dangerous. This wish is, in fact, an incestuous wish. It is the wish to remain mama's big boy and daddy's little princess, even when we surrender ourselves to that most powerful energy that joins the spatial-temporal with the eternal—sexual energy. Safety is an illusion, especially in love.

But if you want to play it safe, if you want to remain a sleeping king or queen, make sure to get yourself a father or a mother as a sexual partner. You should keep in mind, though, that if you want to make love to your father or mother, you will first have to conquer the other parent. In the language of myth, this is called murder.

That is how you, as a sleeping king or queen, kill two birds with one stone: you assume power, and you get a safe sexual partner.

This is the road the isolated *I* will always try to take. It is the road of least resistance. And this is what the oracle meant when it answered Oedipus's question ("From whom do I descend?") so curiously ("You will kill your father and marry your mother."). Translated into the terms of this chapter, the oracle's answer is, "If you identify with your false sense of self, if you maintain that that is your origin, you will kill your father and marry your mother."

From Sleep to Nightmare

Twice now in this myth, the sleeper was called by the voice of life, and twice he didn't open his eyes. He did not break through the boundary of the isolated existence. He stopped in front of what the esoteric literature calls the Guardian of the Threshold.

Then he is called a third time. Now the awakening power enters through the very defenses that the sleeper built up against life: his dreams turn against him. The dark figures who were kept outside the circle of the consciousness advance irresistibly. Life has become a nightmare.

The Guardian of the Threshold

*Its Form was veiled as the face, but the outline
was that of a female; yet it moved not as move
even the ghosts that simulate the living. It seemed
rather to crawl as some vast misshapen reptile.*

EDWARD BULWER LYTTON, *ZANONI*

We will briefly put aside the myth of Oedipus and turn our attention to the extraordinarily important phenomenon of the Guardian of the Threshold. In the next chapter, we will again take up the story of Oedipus.

The Guardian of the Threshold: this mysterious being appears when humans are at the very point of entering a new reality. It is the gatekeeper that asks the password and that tests for truthfulness.

We know it in many forms. In the book of Genesis, it is the sword-wielding cherubim at the gate of paradise "which turned every way, to guard the way to the tree of life." In the Epic of Gilgamesh, it is the feared scorpion man—half man, half dragon—

whom the hero has to pass in his quest for eternal life. In fairy tales it is the giant who bellows at the hero, "Why are you here? Answer quickly, before I turn you into stone." It is an archetypal figure that will exist as long as there are people who follow the path of initiation.

As the power that tests us, it is age-old; as the Guardian of the Threshold, we have known it only since the middle of the last century. It was first brought to the stage by the British author Edward Bulwer Lytton. In his novel *Zanoni,* a monstrous figure addresses one of the main protagonists who wants to embark upon the path of initiation: "Thou hast entered the immeasurable region. I am the Guardian of the Threshold. What wouldst thou with me? Silent? Dost thou fear me? Am I not thy beloved? . . . Kiss me, my mortal lover." Understandably, the protagonist asks for time to think it over, but "the Horror crawled nearer and nearer to him; it crept to his side, its breath breathed upon his cheek! With a sharp cry he fell to the earth insensible, and knew no more."

The name was a real find, and consequently, it stuck. Ever since then, every occult novel has contained a horrible, blubbery anomaly that obstructs the visitor's continuation on the path.

At the end of the nineteenth century, clairvoyants, healers, and spiritual teachers picked up the term and started giving witness to the Guardians of the Threshold they had observed. Some of these were serious observations, but most of them were sensationalistic nonsense. The pinnacle in this land of nonsense was reached by the spiritual teacher Max Heindel, judging by the following clairvoyant observation from *The Message of the Stars,* which he actually penned this down in all earnest:

When we saw the thing, it appeared as a shapeless jellied mass with numerous greenish eyes all over the yellow blob. Every couple of seconds, a sharp swordlike projectile would shoot from some unpredictable spot of its body, and it would penetrate the boy who was lying on his bed, groaning. And even though the monstrosity did not have a mouth to smile with, it appeared to be twitching in malicious joy of the pain and suffering it was inflicting. At other times, one of the eyes appeared to jump out of the monster, as if projected on an elephant-like trunk, and hold still right in front of its victim's eyes, staring at him and holding his gaze with a frightful intensity.

As Heindel reveals to us, this Guardian of the Threshold was the direct result of a secret sexual habit from a previous life.

Before the Law

The best and most concise description of the Guardian of the Threshold was given by a nonoccultist, the writer Franz Kafka. In his short story "Before the Law," he describes succinctly how man wants to go through the gate but encounters the guardian—*his* guardian—there:

Before the Law stands a doorkeeper. To this doorkeeper there comes a man from the country [who] prays for admittance to the Law. But the doorkeeper says that he cannot grant admittance at the moment. The man thinks it over and then asks if he will be allowed in later. "It is possible," says the doorkeeper, "but not at the moment." Since the gate stands open, as usual, and the doorkeeper steps to one side, the man stoops to peer through the gateway into the interior. Observing that, the doorkeeper laughs and says: "If you are so drawn to it, just try to go in despite my veto. But take note: I am powerful. And I am only the least of the doorkeepers. From hall to hall there is one doorkeeper after another, each more powerful than the last. The third doorkeeper is already so terrible that even I cannot bear to look at him." [The man] decides that it is better to wait. The doorkeeper gives him a stool and lets him sit down at one side of the door. There he sits for days and years until he is old and frail and has not very long to live. Before he dies, all his experiences in these long years gather themselves in his head to one point, a question he has not yet asked the doorkeeper. . . . "Everybody strives to reach the Law," says the old man, "so how does it happen that for all these many years no one but myself has ever begged for admittance?" The doorkeeper recognizes that the man has reached his end, and, to let his failing senses catch the words, roars in his ear: "No one else could ever be admitted here, since this gate was made only for you. I am now going to shut it."

If we read this story as a parable, then there is a gate—an opportunity—for every human being that leads to the essence of existence. We could enter without any problems if we would not endow the doorkeeper with powers mightier than our own. Since we do endow it with these powers most of the time, we wait for permission from that which is actually our servant. And to endure the wait, we build up the best possible existence in front of the gate. We pretend that the waiting room is our actual life and we try, very obediently, to make the best of it—until death comes and the gate is shut.

Progress or—to use a different word—initiation only occurs when we do not shy away from that which we project upon the guardian *and* if we give up our attempts at making the best of it in front of the gate.

The Nature of the Guardians

The Guardian of the Threshold is not a figure that stands alone, created by a power outside of us to keep us from going on. The guardian is an archetypal figure, a casing, as it were, that every human being carries with him in his psychological baggage. When we reach an important point of transition, this casing will drop—to extend the metaphor—from our suitcase onto the floor in front of us. We see it lying there and pick it up. This happens almost completely independently of the personal consciousness.

There is something peculiar to that casing: we are fascinated by it, it evokes all kinds of emotions and thoughts in us that we didn't

Guardian of the Threshold, by Jan Uriot

expect to have. It mirrors our fears, our lusts, and our resistance, and it takes on their form. At least, that is how it seems. In reality, it is we who fill it with our fears, lusts, and resistance, like an inflated balloon. That is how we give it life; that is how we give it content. It becomes a figure that rises up in front of us and that grows in size and importance the more seriously we take it. We feed it with our attachment.

The Guardian of the Threshold is, in other words, the materialization of our own ignorance. As such, it represents our past. Everything we have identified with as personality, all the values and opinions from which we have gleaned our identity, hold us back from entering a new realm of life. Yesterday's *I* wants to be tomorrow's *I.* It activates the Guardian of the Threshold; it gives it its peculiar character.

Alice Bailey reaches a very similar conclusion in her book *Glamour: A World Problem:* "The Guardian can be described as the sum total of the forces of a baser nature, as these find expression in our personality before enlightenment, inspiration, and initiation occur." And a little further in the same book, she writes: "The Guardian takes on form when a conscious reorientation, influenced by the soul, has occurred in people's lives; one's total personality is directed at liberation from servitude. The problem is turning theory and inspiration into facts of experience."

Inside and Outside

The following is a dream:

> I arrive at a border town. I walk up to the border crossing. The customs agents of my country let me pass, but the customs agents of the other country won't let me through. It is not clear why I am not allowed to enter the country. They suggest that I have contraband on me. I don't think I did anything wrong. I try reasoning and flattery so they'll let

me into the country but to no avail. Finally, I give up and return to the country I came from. But now, I am not allowed in there, either. I haven't the right papers, they claim. I have to stay in no-man's-land.

One could imagine the guardian being a purely psychic power, an inner resistance that manifests itself in dreams. However, it is more than that. The guardian presents itself equally on the physical as on the psychic level; it inhabits our outside world as well as our inside world.

We can grasp this miraculous phenomenon only when we realize that our inside and outside worlds are directly connected to each other. Everything we think and feel and wish and want has a creative effect on our surroundings, the world in which we live. Our surroundings are the last concretion of our souls. We surround ourselves literally with our surroundings. It is our outer inner world.

In an earlier publication *Echt waar—wensen worden werkelijkheid* (Really True: Wishes Do Come True), we dealt extensively with the creative power we humans possess. We quote:

> Nothing is incidental. Just as your body is the total expression of your possibilities, so are your surroundings. The house you live in is the materialized house of your soul. This is true both for the beautiful vista as well as for the leaking roof.
>
> The winning ticket in the lottery, the accident with your car, your friends and acquaintances, the coffee machine that breaks down, the unexpected meeting, they are all reflections in matter. Even the most minute details. Coincidence does not exist; and because everything— impulse, wish, and resistance—ultimately becomes form, you will bump into it. It isn't a thought or some vague feeling, which you can deny, anymore, it is reality. Because you bump into it, you will have to deal with it. That is the

beginning of self-knowledge and that, in turn, is the beginning of transformation.

"In the past ten years, I've had six bosses, and every time the same thing has happened. It is hard to believe. At first, I really didn't think much of it—I thought, maybe it was just bad luck—but now I see that it could not have been coincidence.

"Whenever I start a new job, everything is fine in the beginning. My boss and I communicate really well. I am given plenty of room to spread my wings, which I do. Everyone is happy. But after a couple of months, just when I feel at home in my job and I am going full steam ahead, the ball drops. Each and every time.

"After a couple of months, I start developing my own ideas and I would like to see them implemented. The ideas are good. My boss thinks so too. He agrees with my ideas in general. But he'll differ on some of the details, insignificant details in the eye of the outsider but important to me. I can't stand that, and I know for sure that I am right. So, I insist. Most of the time, it ends in a row. Sometimes I win an initial confrontation, most of the time I lose—but whether I win or lose, the harm is done. The tension is there. Somehow we never get on the right foot again.

"On the surface, things seems to be going well again, for a while at least. Then something similar happens a couple of months later, with the same result. And then again. And yet again, until it blows up. The scene always ends with me drawing the shorter straw and having to leave. I do feel that, in most of these conflicts, I was right. I lost not because my boss's arguments were better but because he had more power. I have always found that very unreasonable.

"But now, after six times, I am starting to question my role in all of this, because the conflicts were the same, every time, while my bosses were very different from each other."

Thus we meet the Guardian of the Threshold as a real person or a concrete situation in our daily lives. It advances on us in our wakeful life, inescapably, and it appeals to the person we aren't fully anymore at that moment but with whom we still largely identify. It threatens or it seduces or it explains to us very reasonably that we can't do now what we most want. It offers a compromise or it conjures up our future disasters. It comes to us as a physician or a supervisor, as a tax auditor, a partner, or a trusted old friend. We listen, and if we are not careful, we fall under its spell. If that happens, we become immobile and we allow it to determine our lives. It keeps us from making the Great Leap.

This is a good thing because we can only make the leap if we detach ourselves from the messages of the past. Our old *I* cannot enter the New Land. In that high state of energy, it would incinerate.

Dependency

How do we know when we are facing the Guardian of the Threshold? In the first place, we only meet the guardian after a new impulse. The old doesn't satisfy us anymore, and we have gained some insight into the new we desire. The new urges us into a direction we have not gone before.

Consequently, a number of setbacks occur that seem to tell us that what we desire is impossible, that we shouldn't let our wishes guide us, or that we should settle for much less. The opposite is also possible: a strong tailwind pushes us forward, making us believe that all will proceed very quickly. But then the situation constricts into a crisis, often embodied by a single person. This person fascinates us mightily because we are attracted or, on the contrary, repulsed by him. He occupies our minds day and night. All our emotions and thoughts revolve around him. It is as if he is the center of a merry-go-round, of which we are merely one of the seats.

It appears as if it is this person who will effect either our demise or our deliverance. But irrespective of our attraction or our repulsion or both, we are obsessed by it. *Dependency* is the key word in this phase.

If we acquiesce in this dependency, we might feel horrible, but—and this is the strange thing—we might feel safe and satisfied at the same time. We recognize this! In some fashion, we have experienced this before. And by repeating the experience, we are reaffirmed in our self-image. This gives us a feeling of safety, however unpleasant and sad it might be. It is just like an alcoholic who feels safe and satisfied when, after a long period of abstinence, he drinks his first beer again. If we give in to the Guardian of the Threshold, we will always choose the familiar road of least resistance, which, in the end, will prove to be the road of the most resistance.

If we become a mere derivative of the Guardian of the Threshold, our reaction will be a stereotypical one. After all, we dig for an answer to the questions of life from a storehouse of answers we have used many times before. We repeat ourselves, even though it seems that our answer is original.

Under the Tree

The Guardian of the Threshold seduces and threatens, as is exemplified in the legend of the Buddha.

When Prince Gautama—the future Buddha—is meditating underneath a bodhi tree, he is approached by the god Mara, "He Who Kills." The god challenges him and tries to subject him. Mara, who is also Kama ("Lust"), attempts to disturb Gautama's meditation in his two personifications. At first he appears in the form of the most seductive of goddesses, and then, having failed to catch Guatama's attention, he rushes forward in the form of the frightful

Mara. He tries to frighten Gautama with an enormous army. The future Buddha, however, does not interrupt his meditations.

An ancient depiction of this scene shows the sacred tree and, under it, the seat of the Buddha. From one side, the lustful goddesses come in a continuous stream, in all colors and sizes, graceful, voluptuous, and alluring, the fulfillment of every man's dreams. From the other side, the most abject monsters approach— bloodthirsty, ferocious, tusked, and armed with knives, they are living nightmares. Between them is the tree and, at the foot of the tree, the seat. But the seat is empty. The person is gone—no Prince Gautama, no seeker. The seeker has found what he sought: himself, the seeker, the nature of the Buddha. And with it fell away all attachments.

Nothing is left of that which attaches itself to the churning duality offered by the Guardian of the Threshold. Nothing demands to be solved anymore, there is nothing to fear anymore, there is nothing to be satisfied anymore. There is no longer an *I* to accept or reject any aspect of the duality. There is no dependency anymore. The spell is broken. The last guardian is left behind.

Three Forms

The Guardian of the Threshold is a perfect salesman. It has a ready-made sales pitch for every *I*. Appearing in a form that most allures the old *I*, it offers the *I* exactly what he wants to hear. Before the progressing *I* realizes what he is doing, the two peddlers—his old *I* and the guardian—have conned him into a contract for life. In an unguarded moment, he sells, to use the phrase employed in fairy tales, his soul to the devil.

The guardian appears in many forms, as many as there are *I*-forms that want eternal life. A closer look, however, reveals the three basic forms the guardian employs. Two of them we saw earlier:

Mara and Kama, threat and seduction, power and sex, the bearer of death and the bearer of lust. Gautama was not visited by the third one under the bodhi tree because he had met and answered it earlier, when he renounced his family and his wealth. It is the demon of money, the personification of greed, the fear of losing property and the desire to accumulate more.

We know the three forms—power, sex, and possessions—as the most important "foods" of the isolated *I*. Whatever one attaches himself to will determine him. Power, sex, and possessions are the great trinity of the shadow existence, and every Guardian of the Threshold will, negatively or positively, promise us a slew of riches in all three areas. It will promise food or it will threaten to withhold it. It will say, "If you do (or don't do) that, you will be humiliated, you will lose him or her, you will lose your property." Every Guardian of the Threshold will say, "Listen to me in order to get power, sex, and possessions."

Every human being will have to deal with this threesome. They are important not only to people who, by inclination or position, deal with them to an extreme degree. Almost every person has power, even if he is not a corporate or political leader. Anytime we want to keep up appearances—literally or figuratively—we are part of a power struggle. Whenever we don't want to lose face, when it is a case of "all or nothing" or right or wrong, our lives revolve around power. In matters small and large, we exercise negative power if we don't express our true opinions. If we don't let our hearts speak and don't verbalize our truths, we tyrannize ourselves and the people around us.

It is not only recognized rulers who are corrupted by power, and it is not only people with lots of money who are trapped by the desire to accumulate possessions. The moment we want to appropriate something that we are not entitled to, we allow ourselves to be steered by the desire to possess. It happens very often. Isn't it common to think of people who are part of your life (partners, children, and friends) as belonging to you? The closer we are to somebody, the stronger the inclination is to turn that person into an extension of ourselves and to claim that we know what he should or shouldn't do. The desire to possess pushes you to try to make yourself bigger through things (money, cars, houses, or clothing) or other people (interesting people, for example). It is a characteristic of the desire to possess that the possessor ends up being possessed.

Finally, sexuality is a guardian not only for those who visibly have problems with it. Every person who is not absolutely free in matters sexual is the prisoner of this guardian and performs ritual dances for it.

A woman talking about property:

> I once had a great job with excellent benefits and an inflation-proof pension plan. Everything was well taken care of. The only problem was that I didn't like my work very much. It was boring. I wanted to quit, but I couldn't find anything that I liked and that paid as well as that job. My age (I am over thirty) was a negative factor too.
>
> One day, I was offered a job that was everything I ever dreamed of. The work was interesting and exciting, I could learn a lot, and it came with lots of responsibilities. The people for whom I would be working seemed nice and trustworthy. But there was a catch: there was no pension plan, and they couldn't offer me a full-time job. It also meant a slight decrease in salary. My old pension was non-transferable. It made taking the new job a lot riskier.
>
> My friends and family warned me not to change. They fanned my fears and concerns. Yet, I decided to take the new job. I quit my old job.

Then my fears started to haunt me. I lay awake nights. A relative visited me and asked me what was in my employment contract. I didn't have one. He said, "I told you so," and, "What are you going to do without a pension later?" and, "You'll be out on the street."

And indeed, I didn't have anything in writing about my appointment to the position, salary, and the like. With a heart full of fear, I called my future employer. They were very surprised by my worries. I thought, *They must think I'm stupid, now they don't want me anymore.* Anyway, I told them my story and asked for a contract. A couple of days later, it arrived in the mail.

I almost fell into the trap. I almost convinced myself that I had done something very stupid and irresponsible. The warnings of the people around me perfectly matched the inner voices that kept saying, "What about the future if you're not building up a pension?" and, "Something will go wrong, you'll end up penniless."

That was a couple of years ago. Now I know I found the right job. It suits my needs to a T, and it allows me to develop myself more and more. Since I was hired, I have become full-time, and I am making more money than I have ever made.

A woman talking about sex and power:

I am single, but I would very much like to have a relationship with a man. However, that scares me a little bit. To be honest, more than a little bit.

There are times of the year when it is easier to meet new people—that is, men—during vacations. I always look forward to these, and at the same time, I always dread them.

Year after year now, the same thing happens to me. Just before my vacation, I "fall" for somebody. Most of the time, I don't let that person catch on to it; it is much too early for that.

But as a result, all my thoughts are preoccupied with that person during my vacation, and I am not open to others. I tell myself that I don't have to meet other men anymore, and I certainly don't have to fall for somebody. After all, I have somebody that I am falling in love with at home. Maybe.

Hence, I am lending an ear to this voice of fear: "Sex is dangerous, keep away from it. If you really fall in love, you'll lose your head and you'll have to give in. It is better to look at the opposite sex from a distance." My infatuations seem so romantic, but they keep me from fulfilling my heart's desire.

A mother talking about possessions and sex:

It isn't really that bad that my boy is still living at home. I know Frederick is twenty-five already, but we're so happy now. Things are getting better all the time. His father and I are growing a little closer too. How shall I say it? We're becoming best friends. There was a time when that was very different.

No, there isn't any sex anymore. Not in twenty-five years, not since Frederick. We sleep in separate beds. But over the years, that has become a fact we can both live with.

Frederick and I do a lot of things together. We see each other frequently during the day, and I know precisely what he is doing. He likes that. It's just that he isn't doing well at school. And that's because he is so incredibly lazy. He does read a lot, though. It's unbelievable how many books that boy reads in bed.

The other day, he brought a girlfriend home. She is a nice girl, but I think that it is a little too early for them to think about living together. Fortunately, he thinks so too.

The Banking Industry

In addition to individual guardians, there are collective guardians. The guardian of power speaks through politicians and the old triad of church, conscription, and capital. The guardian of sex speaks unabashedly through the porn industry and, more subtly, through the movie industry and scores of other media.

We will not address every one of these guardians here. Everybody knows them. There is, however, one Guardian of the Threshold that operates so imperceptibly that we want to deal with it in more detail. We call this guardian, the one that appeals to our desire to possess, the guardian of the banking industry. This figure lures us in the following manner:

> Are you short of money right now? That is no problem at all. You can get money here. It would be a shame if you didn't take that trip or if you didn't buy the living room set you like so much. Nowadays, you don't have to limit yourself. We are living in a modern age. Everybody can have a line of credit—you too! Go with the times, and don't worry about it. We would love to give you a credit card. If you open an account with us, you'll also get a card with which you can treat yourself to instant cash. With it, you can get money at any ATM. A few years ago that wasn't as easy; now it's a cinch. Evenings, weekends, whenever you need it, you will always have convenient access to money. We are at your service twenty-four hours a day, 365 days a year!
>
> We can line you up with a mortgage too. And even if you have a limited income, come talk to us about mortgages secured by life insurance. It is very simple. Your dream home is a mere signature away. The frugal times are gone. Come and see us for information with no obligation to buy. And in one stop, you can take care of all your insurance and travel needs too. With no money down, you'll drive away in your dream car!

The Angel of the Threshold

One can only pass the individual and collective guardians if he detaches himself from the signals they are transmitting. This does not mean that these signals have to be suppressed. Anyone trying to pass a guardian with his eyes closed is going to be confronted by it again the moment he opens his eyes. In retrospect, the shortest road past the obstacle is the road one takes while fully conscious.

Following is the dream of a man shortly after a very difficult divorce:

> I am in a large castle with lots of corridors. It looks like a labyrinth. I am being chased and shot at from all sides. I try to escape, but I know that is almost impossible; the castle is heavily guarded, everywhere. I run upstairs, and from there, I jump out of the castle. Below me, I see a large moat surrounded by another high wall with a sentinel every couple of feet. While I am falling, I see, in great despair, that escape is impossible.
>
> I land in the moat, but it is not very deep. The water only comes up to my knees. A sentinel looks down at me, and I know that I will be captured again. But I stop running.
>
> I walk straight toward him. I am not afraid of him anymore. I am going to surrender voluntarily. To my surprise, he holds out his hand to me. I put my hand in his, and he pulls me up on the wall. Then, he directs me to a road that leads away from the castle. In addition, he hands me a backpack with what seem to be provisions for the journey. I can hardly believe it, but I take for the road immediately.

The important thing is to acknowledge and recognize the resistance and to go on in spite of it. If one takes to life's path in that way, the Guardian of the Threshold, that dark force, is transformed into a force of light that smiles and bids you a good journey. This greatest of adversaries is not a true adversary. It is a guardian that helps us not to go too fast. It is a helper.

But you can only say this after you have passed it with open eyes. Then, you realize that your whole past—all those *I's* that wanted to remain *I's*—is threaded on a string of love. Only after you have recognized the guardian as a manifestation of the self do you understand that life does not end there. Life goes on and you proceed with it. Life carries you, it poses questions and you answer, but you can not possess the answer.

The guardian will tell you face-to-face that you *can* possess the answer. If you stand still then, you will develop a psychology, a philosophy, a religion, a lasting answer, but you will lose life. After some time—and this could be a lifetime—you'll let go of the security that the system you chose seemed to offer. You start living again.

And what happens to the guardian? Once you go beyond it, you will see that all the images of threat, seduction, and loss were projections onto emptiness, and onto nothing else. It smiles at you. Its smile is your smile. Were you ever somebody else?

seven

The Nightmare

O dark intolerable inescapable night that has no day!
Cloud that no air can take away!
O and again that piercing pain, torture in the
flesh and in the soul's dark memory!

OEDIPUS IN SOPHOCLES' *KING OEDIPUS*

We return to the hero of our story. Oedipus did not pass the Guardian of the Threshold and his life in front of the gate; his life as a king turns into a nightmare.

This always happens if one doesn't pass the guardian. Then the blackness one tries to avoid approaches during the day and during the night. Initially, the blackness appears to be a foreign force, an angry fate that affects others. But gradually it comes closer and closer; one can't escape it. The tension between your ostensible whiteness and the blackness of the apparent evil increases maximally. You are standing on the weaker side, pale, and the blackness wants to destroy you. If it is a bad dream, you wake up with a jolt and you are relieved that it is only a dream—but where did the blackness come from and where is it dwelling now?

We give some examples of nightmares here:

> I am in a large building. It is crumbling all around me. I am trying to get down on some winding stairs. Everything is crashing down. I am terribly scared and start to scream while I am holding on tightly to the newel around which the stairs wind themselves. I wake up screaming.

> I am standing at the edge of a lake. The water stirs. Something is coming out of the water. Something big, enormous. A monster. It resembles a giant lobster. I want to run away, but I can't.

> It is pitch dark. I am in a space, but I can't even see myself. There is a man. He jumps on me. I am fighting. He is stronger than me, but I manage to wrestle him down. I start hitting him hard. He doesn't resist anymore. I manage to get my hands around his neck. I strangle him. His body slackens. Suddenly, I know who I am and who he is. He is my brother. I wake up with a jolt. I sit up straight in bed. I can't sleep anymore.

A nightmare is so intense and the relief afterward so great that the nightmare's "owner" does not easily relate his everyday life to the occurrences of the night. He surfaces from his nightmare, switches on the light, and thinks, *Thank God it wasn't real; it was only a dream.*

Yet, the fear he wakes up with is not just a dream. It is a concretely felt fear that has everything to do with the psyche and the body with which he embarks upon the day. The dreamer and the riser are one and the same person. What he doesn't want to know when awake forces its foot in the door at night; it forces itself in, irresistibly.

The most obvious thing to do is to ask the person having nightmares what he fears most during the day. This can be a first step to reduce the distance between the white of day and the black of night. What is crumbling around him that he fears? Where is he losing his grip on things? What is he desperately trying to hold on to?

When somebody can muster the courage to face what he fears most during the day, nightmares lose their grip. The somnambulic existence of the day comes to an end. But if one refuses to acknowledge what goes on, if one keeps fooling oneself, then the nightmare intensifies. Mercilessly, it will march into one's daily life. What one fears most becomes reality.

The tyrant lives off suppressing, because he continuously has to legitimize his existence. It is precisely in that fighting off that we foil our true liberation.

R. FENTENER VAN VLISSINGEN,
ONDERGANG EN VERHEFFING (DOWNFALL AND ELEVATION)

Our Nightmare

In Oedipus's life, the nightmare begins when his people are plagued by disaster. The citizens of Thebes turn to Oedipus and plead with him to do everything within his power. Oedipus decides to consult the Oracle at Delphi.

Initially, the answer—revenge Laius's death—brings some relief. At least, they now know what to do. But after a while it becomes clear that the bad dream does not go away, it comes closer and closer, and more and more it concerns Oedipus personally. The suffering of the people becomes Oedipus's suffering. When the truth finally hits home, he wants to kill Jocasta, and he pierces his own eyes. The nightmare has become personal reality.

We too are familiar with the nightmare of ever bigger disasters. In today's world, we witness all around us the most dreaded possibilities becoming reality, and they come closer and closer. The problems humanity faces are larger than ever.

One way or another, we have to deal with these problems. But it is not enough to restrict ourselves only to the problems outside of us. We have to deal with the causes also. And that is a much riskier undertaking for us personally, since the causes are found within ourselves.

The voice of the oracle—our inner knowledge—directs us toward the crimes that we committed in our blindness and that led to this nightmare. Whom or what did we kill without knowing it? That is the real question. And if we commit ourselves to answer that question, the nightmare comes closer. It becomes our personal nightmare.

At that point, we can wake up.

Then somebody entered our basement and said, "You'll have to get out, now. The whole house is on fire, any moment it is going to come down." Most people didn't want to, they thought they were safe. They all died. A couple of us did go. It took a lot of courage. We had to crawl outside through a hole and the fire was raging in front of that hole. "It is not as bad as it seems," our messenger said, "after all, I came through it to get to you." Then I wrapped a wet blanket around my head and crawled outside. We got through it. Some of us collapsed on the street. We had to leave the others behind.

HANS ERICH NOSSACK,
DER UNTERGANG (THE DEMISE)

Large and Small

We can relate the Oedipus myth, on a small scale, to our individual lives and, on a large scale, to our collective life— to humanity.

On a small scale, Oedipus is our *I* that seems to have conquered life but, in fact, has shied away from the guardian. The people of Thebes represent our surroundings in which the problems occur. We try to solve them as if they do not concern ourselves.

On a larger scale, we as humanity are Oedipus, and the earth and all its inhabitants are the people of Thebes. Disasters, famine, environmental problems, poverty, overpopulation, epidemics such as AIDS, wars, earthquakes—they seemingly occur outside of us. And we expect to arrive at solutions for these disasters as "good monarchs" would: we change our laws, we levy environmental surcharges, we do research, we send money and goods to stricken areas, we organize aid for the victims, and so on. We human beings do a lot, but always too little to really better the world around us. We fail to see that we ourselves, like King Oedipus, cause these disasters.

We as humanity will not be able to get past the guardian if we merely try to find structural solutions for the results of our negative attitude toward life. We can only get past the guardian if we change our attitude toward life also. To do that, we need to become aware of our own offenses against life, both individually and collectively. We also have to become aware of those offenses and what they cause.

Anything else we do merely treats symptoms. The problems that face us today can be solved only if we become truly different human beings.

Man and Woman

Every Guardian of the Threshold has the power to conjure up horror images for those who want to pass it. This hell will stay with us as long as we shy away from the guardian. In other words, there are as many kinds of nightmares as there are guardians that we believe in.

As we discussed in the previous chapter, the guardian of sex is one of our most fearsome opponents. If we want to become whole again, and if we don't want to remain dependent on our opposite— the other sex—we will have to get beyond this figure. If we stop in front of this guardian's gate, we will inevitably be faced with sexual nightmares indicative of our own form of schizothymia. We will be rejected and humiliated; or we will turn murderous; we'll start hating, possessed by desire or impotency; we'll turn cold and indifferent. All these reactions are possible, but whether we are active or passive, we feel victimized, because, after all, it is a nightmare. It is happening to us.

Mother and Son

Oedipus and Jocasta are these kinds of victims of fate. One can hardly call them guilty of anything. They didn't know that they were mother and son when they entered into marriage. Moreover, they had to become lovers. He was victorious, she was his prize. She was his reward after he had outwitted the Sphinx by answering the riddle. He won a kingdom through his wit; the queen simply came with it.

That was the custom then. But as the truth of the myth makes clear, it is still the case now. Men and women still marry without truly wanting to. They are driven by external and internal forces that are beyond their control. Their friends tell them that they're a perfect couple. He is smart and interesting. She is beautiful and caring. He has a bright career ahead of him, she is from a good family. Everybody agrees: a perfect match. They're made for each other. When he is done with school, everybody urges them—it's about time they get married. A little later, there they are on the stairs in front of a wedding chapel, timidly waving at the guests.

That's the stuff nightmares are made of.

The story continues. He is a man with a rational answer to everything. That impresses her. She looks up to him. Actually, he has only one shortcoming: he is unable to ask for what he needs. But she understands. After all, he is a man who is very much at home in the world, who knows how to get higher up. So, of course, it is hard for him to ask, even for something he really wants.

It isn't always easy to deal with that typical male shortcoming, but it does have its advantages. She uses it to justify their relationship. He is unable to ask, but she can take care of him.

She knows his needs as a mother and she fulfills them. She is there for him, so he can "govern" well. She provides him with food, clothes, children, sexual satisfaction—everything he might need. To do that, she doesn't really need to know him as he really is. She only has to be a mother to him. And for her to take care of him, he doesn't really have to open himself up. He only has to be a good son. She is happy when things are going well for him, when he rises in the world. And he is happy as long as she is there for him. He is the king of the realm in which his "mother" is the queen.

Everything in this relationship revolves around the condition that his knowledge not be touched. And everything revolves around her having no desires.

The System

This is a closed system. Both play their roles and lull each other to sleep. This can go on for years. In the case of Oedipus and Jocasta, it lasted fifteen years.

Then little cracks appear in the system. Then one of them misses a cue. He falls in love with another, or she doesn't put up with his know-it-all attitude anymore. For once, she doesn't want to take care of him. For once, he rejects her care. Or, as in the Oedipus myth, something changes in their surroundings that puts the system under pressure. In a closed system, little changes lead to big shifts. The unity, which seemed so strong, turns out to have no foundation. They have nothing in common that they can hold on to. Their roles disintegrate. Do they have anything left?

Sleep becomes a nightmare. Everything they used to wish for in each other, they now blame each other for. She yells that he doesn't know what intimacy means; he retorts that she doesn't know what letting go means. Day after day. Night after night. It is a living hell.

They are still a system, and one could say that they are conspiring against life. Together they are now the negative of the old positive. Where they used to go along with each other unthinkingly, they now bash each other equally unthinkingly. The difference is now they know that they are in prison together. But even this, the bitterness and the hatred, they could keep up for years. It is, after all, the other's fault. Let *him* change!

A man recounts his nightmare:

> We were married for five years when things turned sour
> between us. I don't know how it started. It happened very
> gradually. I started to feel more and more indifferent
> toward her, and she wouldn't leave me alone. She had
> those dreadful emotional outbursts. She wanted to talk all

the time, and I, on the other hand, wanted to be by myself. We ended up talking, fighting, for days on end. This happened during a vacation, so we had all the time in the world.

I didn't care, no matter what she said. It left me cold as ice. I did find that, very vaguely, kind of annoying. I also didn't think that I was right all the time, but I didn't know any differently. I wanted to keep her at a distance, but I also wanted her to break through that distance—in a good way, a way that was missing constantly. It was a very contradictory feeling. In reality, under all that coldness, I felt despair—although this might be hindsight.

We were both stuck. I couldn't go forward or backward. One day I was sitting in the living room with my head literally in my hands. Suddenly, she came to me, pushed my hands aside, sat on my lap and said, "But I do love you. Let's stop this." For a moment, I melted. In that moment, I could have said yes; instead I pushed her off me and said, "Who has to stop what?"

She went absolutely berserk. She started to scream and ran away. I heard her in the hallway and then the front door slammed shut. I looked through the window. She was outside, no coat, no shoes. This was in the middle of the winter. She was screaming. Hysterical, I thought. I observed the scene as if I were surrounded by Plexiglas. She ran around the house to the kitchen door. I went to the back and I locked the door, just when she arrived there. There we stood, on either side of the glass door. "Hysterical bitch," I said. She kicked through the glass. Pieces of it went flying all over the place. She stepped inside like a fury.

It didn't faze me. She ran to the drawer, took a meat carver, and jumped at me. She stopped right in front of me. It was as if she was doing some ritual dance with the knife. Really, that's what it looked like. I stood with my back against the kitchen door while she slashed through the air. Suddenly, she hit my arm.

At first, I didn't feel anything. Then pain. I touched the spot with my hand. Blood was streaming over my hand. I said, "You stabbed me," surprised. "You'll have to call a doctor." Then I realized what had happened. I went into the hallway, blood gushing onto the stone floor. I heard myself saying, "So it happened after all," very sadly, as if I had known all the time that it might happen. I laid down on the floor, and I tried to compress the artery. I heard her call the hospital. When she put down the receiver, she sat down next to me. We looked at each other. All hatred was gone. Again, I said to her, "So it happened after all." She nodded. We stayed together until the ambulance came.

It was indeed an arterial hemorrhage. We barely made it to the hospital in time. When I was lying on the stretcher, my teeth were chattering, and I shivered all over my body. The nurse thought that it was shock. She said, "Just let it go." That was sweet of her, but it was more than shock. It was my own coldness that I felt. I was melting.

I spent two days in intensive care and then a couple more days in the hospital. I did some hard thinking during those days. It didn't matter anymore whose fault it was. All that time, one thought went through my head: *This is the end.* It was true! The game was up. We couldn't let this happen again. This was the end of the road. I didn't know whether I really loved her, but I remembered very clearly how she had sat with me on the floor when I thought that I was going to die, and how we had looked at each other.

This happened twelve years ago now. We're still together. But our marriage—and we both agree on this— only really started a couple of months after that stabbing. Then we really talked everything through and even stopped talking about things that can't be expressed. Then we forgave each other, and ourselves. Looking back, I can say that only then did I, for the first time in my life, start living with a woman in a mature way, allowing her to see all of me, without the illusion that she has to put things right for me.

Victim and Culprit

What is left when the role one plays is gone—when the play is over?

It is part of your role to think of yourself as a victim of the other, of fate, of life. Inherent in the age-old play of man and woman is that each departs from the notion that one of them is the guilty party and their problems can only be solved if the other takes the first step. Then you realize that the two of you are indeed victims but not each other's victims. You are your own victim! You are both guilty. Neither of you dared to live life to its fullest. Both of you, in the language of the myth, warded off the Sphinx with your superficial intellect, and both of you won the other as a prize because you succeeded.

When, in the end, the Great Sleep turns into nightmare, it is horrible to see how much pain you are able to inflict upon each other. And yet, that is not the worst of it. The worst is that, somewhere deep inside, you realize that you actually knew this from the outset. It is a true feeling of guilt. You not only hurt each other, you hurt life. You let life and all its possibilities go around in old patterns. You turned that completely unknown relationship, which the two of you could have created and which might have ended after a while, into a relationship you already had known for so long: a relationship with your mother or your father or your daughter or your son. Boring and safe. You didn't live. You only repeated. That is the worst. Time marched on, and nothing happened.

Now the question comes: "Is there anything at all between us?" Is all this a mere veneer that has to be peeled back to set free the true relationship, just as with the couple in the previous account? Or were all those years together for the most part only role-playing, and do we have to say good-bye to each other now?

Starting from Zero

If there is little or nothing substantial behind the facade, as with Oedipus and Jocasta; if you were really only mother and son (or whatever roles you were playing), what then? Then you will have to let each other go. But what if you don't want to accept that, don't want to let go, don't want to start from zero? Then the nightmare will drive you to the final stage, and there you will either go under or wake up.

In the myth, we witness Oedipus tearing through the palace in rage. "A sword, a sword," he cries. "Where is that wife, no wife of mine—that soil where I was sown, and whence I reaped my harvest?" He wants to kill her, as if she were the cause of his agony. He is still the son. He is furious at his mother, because she betrayed him.

While thinking about this scene, we almost automatically relate it to the encounter with the Sphinx. Oedipus knew how to ban this mysterious female figure from his life by employing reason. The Sphinx threw herself off the cliffs, screaming. But did she really die? Didn't she return into his life in the form of Jocasta, as some commentators have suggested?

Whatever the answer may be, Oedipus tries to cut Jocasta out of his life. She beats him to it, however: she takes her own life. Some claim that the shame was too much for her, but there is more to it than that. At least, that is how it appears if we identify with her. She was always willing to do anything for him, as a mother. She sacrificed all her own desires. And now it is apparent that all was for naught. For naught. He is not her partner. There is a large gaping hole where she assumed the partner to be. She killed her desires, for an illusion. There was nothing left, except the one desiring. Now she has killed that one too. Otherwise she would have had to go into the void, just like Oedipus.

Oedipus unties the rope with which she hanged herself and lays her on the ground. Then he pierces both his eyes with the golden brooches of her dress. Now that he sees what Teiresias saw, he too has become blind.

This is the high point of the nightmare. Here Oedipus begins to wake up. His knowledge is broken. Now he begins the journey that leads to initiation. For the first time, he consciously allows a woman to lead him. Antigone—daughter and sister in one—goes before him and leads him by the hand. She leads him out of the nightmare.

We shall follow Oedipus on this road. But, in the next chapter, we will first take a closer look at the helper who led him into the nightmare, the blind seer Teiresias.

eight

Help and Helpership

They are bringing the prophet in whom,
of all men, lives the incarnate truth.

CHORUS IN SOPHOCLES' *KING OEDIPUS*

Just as a fish is not aware that it lives in the water, we don't know that we are surrounded and permeated by life, and that life is help. Insofar as we identify with our personalities, we are blind for not wanting to see. As limited personalities, we are able to observe the outside of things, analyze them, and compare them with other outsides, but we are blind to the living essence. We see, but we don't see that we are seeing. We are staring blindly at our suspicions and expectations, and we are torn between hope and fear. Yet, all that time, the knowledge is there, sparkling in the depth of our existence. All our questions have been answered already. Life surrounds us, carries us, and feeds us. There is nothing to fear. All is help.

As limited personalities, we fear help most of all. Help demands that we let go of all our preconceptions and that we be willing to receive. The personality does not want to receive, it wants more of the same.

If we had an eye for it, we would be able to see that the paths of our lives are marked by help refused and misunderstood. So much is given to us, and so little accepted.

From whence comes the light when dreaming?

HANS ERICH NOSSACK,
UNMÖGLICHE BEWEISAUFNAHME (THE IMPOSSIBLE PROOF)

Dreams

There is help day and night. Liquid light streams through the darkness of sleep and coalesces into forms and figures that touch us. Our dreams offer us a helping hand. They invite us to step into the light. They help us by giving form to our wishes and resistances on our inner stage. They show us what lives in us and what we keep hidden from ourselves. Dreams reveal our trivialities, the peculiarities of our personalities, and their consequences. But in the end, they reveal our greatness, and they help us flow into who we really are. They help us to converge with the light that we always were— that we are.

When we wake up from our dreams, most of the time the solidification into a personality occurs again when we say, "Oh yes, it is me. This is my name. This is how I feel. This is how I think. This is how I act. What was I doing again?" Maybe, the personality might see, as in a flash, the dreams it dreamed, although it was not dreaming then. And then after the personality looks at the dreams in surprise for a moment or two, it proceeds with its daily chores again and lets the dreams fade away.

Every dream is help, but the help is not unconditional. We have to free ourselves from our *I*-restriction. If we want to receive help, we have to tune in to it. We have to be willing to make a sacrifice.

Then, we can learn from our dreams. Then, we can pose our deepest questions to our dreams. If we recognize that we are blind in seeing and if we are willing to follow the track of light, the dreams will accept us as apprentices.

A man is dreaming. He is forty-five years old, extremely unhappy in his job, but for reasons financial and other, he doesn't dare to quit:

> I am sitting in my office at my desk. My wife and children are there too. Before me is a stack of files. As so often in the last couple of years, I am blindly staring in front of me, desperate. Suddenly, the walls of my office fall away. My desk is gone too. Around me, I see an infinite expanse. My wife and children are with me. I look down. We are sitting on a hand, a giant hand that encloses and holds us. I wake up thankful, touched. I know, without a shadow of a doubt, that I will quit my job.

The Master

Just as in our nighttime dreams, there are figures of light in our daytime existence, too, that come toward us. They are the help of life, the incarnate truth. This truth is blind to the laws of our surface existence; it sees, again and again, the causality of our agony and the royal path of liberation that leads out of the agony. This is the blind seer.

This help also demands something from us before we can receive it. It is not poured into us. We have to learn to tune in the receiver—which our personality can be—to the frequency in which the help is broadcast. This tuning in demands sacrifices and exertions. It demands a reversal of us, a different disposition. We are attuned if we "take up our bed and walk," as the Bible says. As soon as we don't lie down passively in our own structure anymore, help can reach us.

Those who have risen, like Jesus of Nazareth and Prince Gautama, allowed themselves to be "overpowered" by figures of pure light like the Christ and the Buddha. When the apprentice has found the master, the apprentice-master separation is eliminated. They are one. The personality that has found its master enters into an apprenticeship. It takes the path of trial and, consequently, the path of initiation. On this path, it detaches itself from its self-images and becomes a master itself.

This doesn't end the apprenticeship, just as the mastership never actually started. Every human being is apprentice *and* master. Every human being is light playing with light. When inner eyes are closed to light, a "somebody" emerges who is blind in seeing. But the light plays on. It doesn't know any darkening. Where inner eyes are closed, our counterpart—the blind seer—enters from the outside world.

From the multitude, a single figure will come forward in our lives, a figure that shows us the path, the path that is no path, because we ourselves are it. This figure is the master of our lives.

The more we come face-to-face with him, the more we experience that we converge with him. The inner blindness is lifted. Through him we experience that all help, all the road markers we followed in our lives—the dreams of the night, the friends, the lovers, our teachers, our parents—converge into a stream of light, the light we have always followed, the light that we are. Gustav Meyrink writes about this helper figure in his initiation novel *The Green Face:*

> I couldn't take my eyes off him, and his face became more
> and more familiar, until I suddenly realized that not a
> single night in my life had gone by without my seeing him
> in my dreams. I gradually went back through my memory

(I wanted to find out when I had seen him for the first time), and my whole childhood seemed to unroll before my inner eye: I saw myself as a tiny baby, and then before that, as a grown-up in a previous existence that I had never suspected, and then as a child and so on and so on; but every time he was with me.

Oedipus and Teiresias

In the Oedipus myth, Teiresias, the blind seer, is the master who reveals to Oedipus that he is blind in seeing. That truth is not accepted without resistance. It is a dramatic confrontation, in which Oedipus tries everything to depose Teiresias and to discredit him, just as we, to the extent that we identify ourselves with our personalities, will do everything not to have to accept the help offered and the truth that is made visible by it.

The dialogue between Oedipus and Teiresias is a fascinating dialogue between somebody who demands help but doesn't want to hear the answer, and the bearer of the truth.

Initially, Oedipus beseeches Teiresias with an urgent request for help, and Teiresias asks in every possible way to be spared having to give an answer. Oedipus increases the pressure; he threatens, is enraged, shows contempt, claims to be insulted, and finally he even accuses Teiresias: "If you had eyes to see with, I would have said your hand, and yours alone, had done it all."

Then Teiresias reveals the truth: "You are the cursed polluter of this land." Oedipus is furious. Teiresias goes on and proclaims, "I say the killer you are seeking is yourself." Like an angry child, Oedipus accuses him (and everybody around him) of anything that comes to his mind, from ignorance to fraud and power games, and he ridicules Teiresias's blindness. Teiresias, however, sticks to his words and pronounces what he knows about the past, the present, and the future. He stays detached and doesn't answer Oedipus's accusations. His last words are: "Go in, and think on this. When you can prove me wrong, then call me blind."

The truth has to be told regardless of the person and no matter what the consequences. That is why the symbol of Justice is blindfolded; that is why the seer Teiresias is blind.

The classic dialogue between the bearer of the truth and the person who is and isn't asking for help because his life has become a nightmare is heard nowadays too, in many forms and on many levels.

The nightmares are horrible, but the consequences of facing up to the truth appear to be even more horrible. Enormous ego interests are at stake, which explains the excessive vilification, the subversion, and the suppression of those who speak the truth. The present nightmare is that we, as humanity, apparently cannot survive; the price that the Teiresiases of our time demand of us is that we give up our "absolute kingship" and again become an integral part of the living whole of this planet.

The Truth as Answer

In the Oedipus myth, Teiresias does not crumble. This is, however, not always the case with the bearer of the truth. He may find many a pitfall on his path. In the biblical myth of Jonah, the story of Jonah and the whale, these pitfalls are exemplified in detail. On first sight, the story in its entirety seems to be nothing but pitfalls.

Jonah is called upon by God to preach to the inhabitants of the city of Nineveh because, as God says, "their wickedness has come up before me." Jonah fears the reaction of the inhabitants of Nineveh and flees. He boards a ship to go as far away from God and from Nineveh as possible. But God "hurled a great wind upon the sea, and there was a mighty tempest on the sea, so that the ship threatened to break up." It becomes clear to the mariners that Jonah is fleeing from his God and that they will only be spared if they cast him overboard. "So they took up Jonah and threw him into the sea; and the sea ceased its raging."

Jonah and the Whale, in the Bible from Heisterbach, circa 1240, Keulen

Once he is in the sea, a great fish—the "whale"—swallows up Jonah. For three days and three nights, he is in the belly of the fish, and in that darkness, he prays. In his prayer, he praises God and vows to do God's bidding, whereupon God speaks to the fish, and it vomits Jonah onto the dry land.

Now Jonah does proceed to Nineveh to preach. Once there, he announces in accordance with God's word that the city will be overthrown in forty days because of the sins committed by the citizens of Nineveh.

Jonah's words have an unexpected effect. The citizens of Nineveh do not kill Jonah, as he had expected. They don't harm him; they don't even ridicule him. On the contrary, they take his message in all earnest and turn from their evil ways. They repent. God, upon seeing that they truly repent, decides to spare Nineveh.

"But this displeased Jonah exceedingly, and he was angry." He complains to God, because he finds it unacceptable that his prophecies will not come true. He exerted himself enormously to reach Nineveh, he risked life and limb, and he foretold, with great assertion, the overthrow of Nineveh. And now it is not going to happen? He was made a fool.

In the end, however, God explains to Jonah that what is important is not the things he prophesied coming true, but what happens on account of his prophesying. If the people of Nineveh better their lives because they truly listened to what Jonah had to say, they don't deserve punishment, but mercy.

One at a time, all the pitfalls of the divine messenger are explicated in this myth. Initially, there is the fear of what others will say and the flight to escape the dreaded task. When a storm comes up in life and what one thought of as an escape is in danger of being shipwrecked, it is hypocrisy to maintain that one doesn't know what has caused this storm in one's life (although Jonah didn't go that far). Then, when all moorings have fallen away, there is the desperate and rancorous sinking away in depression, "in the dark belly of the large fish." (Jonah didn't go that far, either; instead he prayed and meditated and bound himself anew, even in his deepest darkness, to the source of light.) Finally, there is the arrogance to think that one's prophecy has to come true, as if that were more important than people changing their lives for the better.

What is more important in the end? To tell the truth and thereby pass judgment in the realm of cause and effect, or to react to a negative impulse, allowing for the redirection of that impulse? The latter, of course! The latter is intervening at germination, which allows for the good to grow. The first—decreeing with a holier-than-thou satisfaction that things have gone irrevocably awry—has nothing to do with verity; on the contrary, it merely evidences the self-importance of the bearer of the truth.

The Two Figures

Inside of us, we all know both Oedipus and the blind Teiresias. The two are closely linked. It is difficult to hear the truth, but it is also difficult to convey the truth. Only he who can bear the truth about himself is allowed and able to tell the truth to another.

The Oedipus figure within ourselves can be illustrated by an alcoholic admitting his drinking to a counselor at a treatment center:

> Right now, I drink about two twelve-packs a night, and then, during the day, an occasional drink here and there. Most of the time everything's okay, though lately a few problems have come up. My kids have started to avoid me, and my wife started sleeping on her own. I maxed out my credit cards, and a while ago I lost my job. I want to do something about it now, 'cause twenty-four beers every night, well, it *is* a bit much. Of course, a few beers won't hurt. Those don't make me aggressive. They told me that you can help me; that's why I'm here.

It is evident from conversations with alcoholics and other addicts that almost no one who enters treatment wants to stop drinking, but rather wants to drink *less.* During the course of the treatment, it gradually becomes clear to the alcoholic that the crucial factor is *never* to drink a drop of alcohol again. This truth always hits the addict like a bolt of lighting during the one-to-one relationship with a counselor, who, at the right moment, reveals the full truth. Every former addict remembers that precise moment.

Hence, the resulting insight is not gained through some methodical treatment that is generally applicable, but through a personal confrontation in which the truth is told and heard.

Every person experiences daily how difficult it is to admit the truth. Whether in an appointment you'd rather not take, work you don't like, a relationship in which you don't feel free anymore, you do A, but you would much rather do B; you accept a proposal although you know that it is not what you want. You keep ending up with compromise solutions that hover in your head like a heavy fog, until you get used to that also.

The truth demands a loving radicalness that, at first, is usually not accepted in gratitude. But you don't tell the truth to please somebody. The truth passes through you and has to be told as the only possible answer you can give to the people with whom you are dealing.

If you want to be both Oedipus and Teiresias—if, in other words, you want to hear and pass on the truth—you are a helper.

Ever since, I could say, I have my heart in my head,
and my brains in my chest.

GUSTAV MEYRINK, *THE GREEN FACE*

Nobody Excepted

There is no such thing as a special "race of helpers," a particular group of people one either belongs to or not, no more than creativity is a special talent some people have and others don't. In essence, every human being is a helper. Everybody is familiar with the spontaneous urge in his life to help another.

Initially, you experience this spontaneous urge in spurts, when, in times of emergency, somebody appeals to your compassion very strongly. That is the moment you become cognizant of your essence and of the insignificance of the things you usually deem important.

For example, a dear friend suddenly falls ill. It is a severe illness, and it is likely that he will only have a short time to live. At that moment, you suddenly seem to possess an enormous potential of love and strength. You are touched to the very bottom of your soul, and you do everything possible to be there for that person. Of course, you call up the deepest resources inside of you. All thoughts of tomorrow fall away; it is crucial for you to be there now. You act with perfect efficiency because you are tuned in to what the situation demands. The personality, in actualizing your loving self, assumes a modest place. And however serious the situation might be, you feel that you are living life to its fullest, you feel completely at home in it. It is completely natural for you to give your absolute best.

You might not have realized that a decision, a decree of the will, lies at the origin of your pure being. You made that decision in a split second, and you relayed it inward: "I am going to give my all, because this is a matter of life and death." Your will is backing up the fact that this is the most important thing in your life. All those other things that normally occupy your mind, considerations about the future or preoccupations with the past, seem futile now. Then you notice that a spontaneous inner movement follows this resolve of the will: the loving engagement of your personality. The help is there immediately. Inwardly, you have come home.

Every human being is a helper, as soon as he knows in his heart and feels in his head that it comes down to the now, that this is the moment.

Helpership as Creativity and as a Link in a Tradition

As illustrated, the basis of helpership is the inner urge to help others. It is sometimes suggested that this alone is enough, that one would only have to follow one's impulses and all would fall into place. But it takes more than inspiration to be a good helper.

All those who have devoted themselves to the service of humanity have, over the centuries, laid the foundation for a tradition—a tradition with rules and regulations. These rules and regulations comprise a totality of concentrated knowledge that is based in experience. Every helper will have to draw from his own experience to truly provide expert help. Otherwise his help will be diluted by something that he hasn't worked through himself, and parroted knowledge doesn't help anyone. And yet, the helper will have to anchor himself in the existing knowledge.

Living help entails knowing that the process of becoming whole always takes place in accordance with certain rules. For example, helping is knowing that the phenomenon of "transference" always occurs where help is offered, knowing how to recognize that, and knowing how to avoid it. When you honor the tradition, you as helper acknowledge that you are assimilating a thought that, a long time ago, was employed by helpers equally inspired and with the same love for the process as you feel. You will have to develop that thought further on your own.

Cardinal Rules of Helpership

There are three cardinal rules of helpership within our tradition. Every person who follows the path of consciousness development will have to deal with these. They make clear in a simple fashion what temptations are lurking most for those wanting to help others.

1. *Nobody can help another. You help yourself—or you don't. Everything else is mere illusion and delusion.*

The effects you have as a helper you have only insofar as you heal yourself. Outside of that, there is no effect. You are the *instrument* for the healing power of love. You don't *do* the healing. That is why helping is "only" a matter of your being prepared to open up to a force bigger than you are as an individual and to offer yourself to that force with your whole personality. This is called attunement.

You are connecting to the negative pole of the earth with your feet and to the positive pole of heaven with your head. Thus, you become a force field. You take the other into this field, address him, and follow every impulse that comes up inside of you, completely trusting that this is help. Period. Whatever happens next is salutary for you as a person. You open up to life completely. You don't know the next step. You keep nothing for yourself.

Evidently, no helper escapes the temptations to think of himself as healing and helping another. Every helper has a personality, and everybody wants to feel important. This doesn't mean that you can become a helper only when you have become totally unselfish. Your total purity is not important; your intention is. Do you think it more important for you to "listen" than to do "good"? Are you accountable for that? Do you hold yourself up against the light?

The touchstone is to be relaxed. If you are tense, you withdraw from the situation. You haven't opened up because you think that something special should occur, or because you think that you have to do something special.

The most important thing you learn as a helper is the difference between being special and being normal. The wish to help others is the strongest motive to bring to light every illusion of the human personality. This is very understandable, since we are dealing with the art of turning lead into gold. We are dealing with the most desirable state in our universe: light, love, and happiness. When you have the tools to bring about that state, you have at your disposal the greatest power in the world. Hence, all one's pride and every fantasy of grandeur are activated.

The helper who takes this first rule seriously is learning to follow his impulses based in relaxation. This is only possible in humbleness.

2. *You are the center of your field and you fulfill your field; the resistance you encounter there is your own resistance.*

When you attune yourself, at the beginning of a discussion, for example, you do this by directing yourself as much as possible to the stream of light and love that you know, in heart and in mind. Phrased differently, you let as much light and love in as your personality can possibly contain. Then you deploy everything you have in you. You consciously plot a field. Your emanation becomes as you wish it to be, and you are the center of it. There is nothing more you can do.

Next, you have to make sure to stay attuned and not leave your center. The criteria is whether you keep feeling free, alive, and light while you relate to the other. The moment you start worrying about what is going to happen, the moment you start considering what the next step should be, something is wrong with you. This is always a sign that a resistance of your personality is coming into play.

This isn't bad, as long as you recognize it as such. You are then able to tell yourself, "This is something about me, this has nothing to do with the other, so if I follow this path, I'll end up in a dead end. I should let go of it and attune myself afresh with renewed courage. I'll pay attention to this resistance of mine later." You let go, you attune yourself again, and the process can continue.

If, however, you proceed as if nothing is the matter, or as if this resistance really does concern the other and not you, you will lose touch, more and more, with the reality of the here and now. Then you are not the initiator anymore in a real connection; instead, you have become a derivative of your personal resistance. You become defensive or aggressive or coercive. In any case, you aren't freely in touch with your life source anymore. This can't be kept up for long, because you will feel more and more troubled and unreal. Yet, it is very difficult to stop such a negative process and to admit to yourself that you have become entangled in it.

Psychologically speaking, this is a case of "countertransference," when you as the helper lose the initiative. Within the helper-worker relationship, it is crucial to allow the other into your field 100 percent and for you to stay completely disinterested. Every time you want to help the other or you close yourself off from him, you leave your center. As helper you will get ample opportunity to experience how exactly you fear your inadequacies.

The helper who takes this second rule seriously in real life situations perceives that he has chosen the path of the fighter, the player, the artist, and the healer.

3. *Uninteresting resistances—that is, resistances you don't know or that have no appeal to you—have to be removed.*

In the previous rule, the important factor was to recognize your own resistance and not regard it as the other's. Once you realize that you are prepared, come what may, to look at yourself in this manner with all your faculties of judgment and to act accordingly, you are able to vouch for yourself. Then the people around you can rely on you. You know the shortcomings of your personality and you don't allow yourself to be determined by them. When you are able to do that, you can live up to the third rule: to confront the other if he does not act in accordance with his better knowledge.

What we are dealing with here is the art of continuing to express yourself, whatever this might invoke in the other. It demands that you as helper are answerable for the power you have. This is not the power of the authority who knows what is good for the other. It is an inner power that hails from the fact that you are prepared to connect permanently with your essence and that you are not going to give in to difficulties.

It is the helper's function to teach his charge to lead his life in accordance with his own inner conscience. The demand on the helper is to express his vision precisely and to vouch for it with his own way of life. In other words, everything the helper does and does not do is open to criticism.

The helper continuously exposes old forms. In this sense, he is a pioneer. Because of this he creates a resistance within those who are willing to compromise more than he is. This kind of work is radical and difficult. On the one hand, you are doing what you know is right; on the other hand, you will have to learn not to let yourself get bogged down in the resistance that those whom you are influencing are inevitably going to direct at you.

The sole criteria here is, again, "Am I committed with all my heart, do I keep following the life within myself freely?" If you stick to that, you will be able to distinguish whether the resistance you experience in the other concerns you too—in which case you will become muddled (as in the second rule)—or whether the other is resisting because he refuses to give up something.

In the latter case, you are impeding progress if you attribute the resistance to yourself. Instead you should make it clear to the other that he is dealing with resistance, that he is not willing to face something essential. In other words, he is engaging in transference, instead of engaging himself. This demands your complete devotion, because you know that sparks will fly when you address the issue. Will he do it or won't he? If he does it and accepts the truth, we can proceed. If he won't, and persists in the resistance, you have no alternative but to remove the resistance from your field. This can indeed mean asking the person to leave. No one demands any heroism from you.

This can only be accomplished with no feelings of guilt or failure when the helper is aware that he is a mere instrument of the great source of help. The world doesn't come to an end just because the person who came to you for help breaks off contact with you. The important thing is for you to act in accordance with your knowledge. You are not the only one who can heal and help.

The helper who takes this third rule seriously experiences that whoever wants to spare the other pain, becomes loveless.

Teiresias, the Bearer of Peace

This third rule is fully applicable to the confrontation between Oedipus and Teiresias. Initially, Teiresias wants to spare Oedipus the pain, but then he realizes that nothing can be avoided. He speaks the truth and is opposed by all of Oedipus's negative force.

In order to feel, as a reader, the incredible tension Oedipus feels at that moment, you have to follow the myth from within. It demands that you do not place Oedipus's tragedy outside of yourself, but that you are willing to discover it within yourself. As a man you apparently wish—besides all kinds of other wishes—to possess your mother sexually, and the same is true for a woman in relation to her father. A man will want to kill his father, a woman her mother. It is very difficult to allow these possibilities into your consciousness, let alone to allow them to get through to your feelings. Difficult and scary, but not inhuman.

When you are able to admit that these urges are present within you, Oedipus gains your sympathy, and you also understand his resistance to the truth and his rage toward Teiresias. You hope—just as a child would—for a miracle that would shield him from the full impact of the terror. We hope for such miracles ourselves, when we have a secret we think of as bad and of which we are deeply ashamed.

However, when Jocasta tries to convince Oedipus to let it go and not to pursue the truth, Oedipus replies: "I must pursue this trial to the end, till I have unraveled the mystery of my birth. . . . I am the child of Fortune, the giver of good, and I shall not be shamed. . . . Born thus, I ask to be no other man than that I am, and will know who I am."

This we recognize too. Deep in your heart, you realize that happiness is yours when you truly know who you are. The desire to experience that is stronger than the hope that the cup will pass you.

It is the desire that, at some point, you will succeed in revealing your total self, and it is the longing for the peace that results from it. Undoubtedly, it is also the desire to come into contact with a Teiresias.

You want to spare Oedipus the painful denouement, but you only find true relief when the truth is revealed and when Oedipus finally gives in to it. Then things "do not turn out for the better after all." There is no happy ending, which is good, because we didn't really hope for that. An integral part of the wish is for you to be able to bear the agony, which you have always feared, and for you to become wise and light because of it.

This is how we know that Teiresias is a good helper. He not only helps Oedipus relieve his conscience, but also helps him to reach his naked self. He brings peace.

nine

The Full Emptiness

Tell me, Antigone—where have you come to now with
your blind old father? What is this place, my child?
Country or town? Whose turn is it to-day to offer
a little hospitality to the wandering Oedipus?
It's little I ask, and I am well content with less.

OEDIPUS IN SOPHOCLES' *OEDIPUS AT COLONUS*

Visibly blind to everyone, Oedipus enters his exile. Unlike Teiresias, his inner eye hasn't opened yet. He is totally blind. Antigone leads him by the hand. His power, his possessions, his popularity, the wife he loved—he has lost it all. He has only himself and his memories. But even his memories offer little comfort. On the contrary.

Who is he? What made him deserve this? There is no answer, nothing that satisfies or distracts. All that exists is total emptiness, and in it, pain is the last remnant of self-awareness.

In the emptiness, the pain very slowly dissolves. It takes years, but in the end, the memorable moment arrives in which Oedipus speaks of himself as "a holy man, and by holy ordinance my presence here is to bring this people blessing." What follows is a final confrontation with his family members, the past he leaves behind. The deity is calling for him; there is nothing that binds him anymore. He goes from a painful emptiness into an emptiness in which self-awareness—be it negative or positive—is not the focal point anymore. He leaves the earth behind and is taken up into the mystery. The chorus chants: "This is the end of tears; no more lament. Through all the years immutable stands this event."

An Experiment

Emptiness. What is emptiness? Much can be said about it, but let us first venture an experiment that could take us beyond words. It is an experiment involving the faculty of imagination—a guided imagery.

> Imagine, reader, that you are stone-deaf. You no longer hear anything, neither from outside of your body nor from inside your body. Total silence.
>
> Imagine next that you no longer smell anything. Smell no longer exists. And with the loss of your olfactory sense, your sense of taste is gone. Sweet, salty, bitter, sour—none exist anymore.
>
> Imagine then that you can no longer move. You are paralyzed from head to toe. You also don't have any bodily sensations anymore. You can't talk, and you don't feel anything, not even your breathing.
>
> Now your vision is your only connection with the outside world. Finally, imagine that you are blind.
>
> Stay in this state for some time.

If you are following these directions carefully, you probably aren't able to read that last sentence. You are in a state of complete sensory deprivation, although there is no way of explaining this to you as long as you are in that state. It is possible that you like this state so much that you stay in it from now on. In that case, you will never read this passage or the rest of the book. It is also possible that you will "open" your senses again after a certain time. Then you will start reading again.

Let us assume the latter. Now we can talk about your experiences during this state of complete sensory deprivation. Even though you did not receive any stimuli from your senses, you did in all probability experience some things. You had thoughts, you felt, perhaps you even "saw" all kinds of things. If the experiment was a success, there was no outside anymore—there was emptiness—but you were probably far from experiencing emptiness inside.

By using one's faculty of imagination in this manner, one detaches oneself from sensory perceptions. It is as if he says, "I am not my senses. Even if I can't communicate through my senses, I still exist." When one disconnects his senses, the attention shifts to the inner world. He will experience more strongly his thoughts and feelings. He probably will also get in touch more with inner sensations such as inner vision or inner hearing. This does not mean that he is freer now, because these thoughts, feelings, and sensations can possess him just as much as the sensory perceptions did earlier. He isn't beyond attachment. What has occurred is merely a shift in the stress of the attachment. He keeps on filling the emptiness with thoughts and feelings that try to maintain themselves, as if they had lives of their own.

We could say that you can only speak of an unconditional state of emptiness if you are able to close off your feelings and thoughts too. Then you would be free. You would no longer be possessed by any kind of image of yourself as an isolated *I*. That is the great liberation.

Lilly's Tank

The above guided fantasy resembles scientific experiments with sensory deprivation conducted in the last thirty-five years. One of the first researchers in this field, the U.S. scientist John Lilly, has the following to say in his book *The Center of the Cyclone:*

> Previous neurophysiologists . . . had hypothesized that the brain stayed in a waking state because of external stimulation coming through the end organs of the body. In other words, outside stimulation was necessary in order to maintain the brain in an awakened state. The obvious experiment was to isolate the human from all external stimulation insofar as this was physically possible, and to see what the resulting states were:
>
> I decided that the way to do it was to float in water using a head-mask in order to breathe and to be in neutral buoyancy within the water so as to attenuate gravity effects. At the same time all sound was to be cut off from the person suspended in the water, all temperature differences over the body were to be attenuated as far as possible, all light was to be cut off, and all stimulating clothing was to be removed.

In the isolation tank, Lilly first discovered that he absolutely did not feel the urge to fall asleep. He found that it didn't take any external stimulation to stay awake. He could have concluded his research with this observation, but he went further. He had all kinds of experiences and started to investigate those:

I went through dreamlike states, trancelike states, mystical states. In all these states, I was totally intact, centered, and there. At no time did I lose conscious awareness of the facts of the experiment. Some part of me always knew that I was suspended in water in a tank in the dark and in silence.

I went through experiences in which other people apparently joined me in this dark silent environment. I could actually see them, feel them, and hear them. At other times, I went through dreamlike sequences, waking dreams as they are now called, in which I watched what was happening.

He who restrains his organs of action but continues in his mind to brood over the objects of sense deludes himself and is said to be a man of false conduct.

But he who controls the senses by the mind, O Arjuna, and without attachment engages the organs of action in the path of work, he is superior.

THE BHAGAVAD GITA, III: 6, 7

A Second Experiment

Lilly noticed—just as everybody does who starts with meditation and detaches himself regularly from the outside world—that the inner world is at least as impressive and moving as the outside world. He proceeded to investigate his inner world, although we will not follow him in his search here. We intend to go one step further, and we will try to answer the question, What happens if you detach yourself not only from your sensory perceptions but also from your feelings and thoughts?

Let us try to formulate a first answer to this question with another personal experiment:

> Imagine, reader, that you do not have any sensory perceptions. Next, perceive your feelings and thoughts. Notice that you feel them and that you think them; detach yourself from them. If they are still in your inner space, regard them as possibilities, as feelings and thoughts that don't concern you. Detach yourself and be who or what you are. Who or what are you?

The first experiment demanded a great degree of effort and concentration. This second experiment demands more, much more. It demands—and this might sound strange—nothing.

Everything you do and bring to bear, every psychological effort, is food for your feelings and thoughts. Only when you do "nothing" are you not maintaining your old feelings and thoughts and not creating new ones. Then the true nature manifests itself.

This does not mean that the crucial point is to be passive. Passivity is still a form of activity. The point is that you are free from what you are doing, whatever that doing entails. You converge with the deed, but you are not attached to it. That is what the Taoist Chinese call *wu-wei* (not-acting, letting go.)

Chuang Tzu, the great Chinese sage who lived some three centuries B.C., speaks of this throughout his writings, which sparkle with wit. The third book, "The Secret of Caring for Life," tells of a master cook who explains to Lord Wen-Hui how he does his work:

> "What I care about is the Way, which goes beyond skill. When I first began cutting up oxen, all I could see was the ox itself. After three years I no longer saw the whole ox. And now—now I go at it by spirit and don't look with my eyes. Perception and understanding have come to a stop and spirit moves where it wants. I go along with the

natural makeup, strike in the big hollows, guide the knife through the big openings, and follow things as they are. . . .

"A good cook changes his knife once a year—because he cuts. A mediocre cook changes his knife once a month—because he hacks. I've had this knife for nineteen years and I've cut up thousands of oxen with it, and yet the blade is as good as though it had just come from the grindstone. There are spaces between the joints, and the blade of the knife has really no thickness. If you insert what has no thickness into such spaces, then there's plenty of room—more than enough for the blade to play about it. That's why after nineteen years the blade of my knife is still as good as when it first came from the grindstone. . . ."

"Excellent!" said Lord Wen-Hui. "I have heard the words of Cook Ting and learned how to care for life!"

The master cook performs his job with no effort of the will. He is on the cutting edge of inner and outer worlds, and he is free to enter both.

When you are not determined anymore by either the inside or outside, you are free to go in or out. But it is not "you" anymore that is going. There is no *I* anymore that wants, above all, to live its own life and that is forced to follow the patterns of its conditioning. Freedom reigns. Everything is possible. Nothing is determined through a past or through a vision of the future. There is emptiness—not a "hollow" emptiness, but a "full" emptiness.

The heart of those that are called is silent.
That is why it is the mirror of Heaven and Earth.

CHUANG TZU, BOOK 13, "THE WAY OF HEAVEN"

Building and Surrendering

In the second experiment, one can get a taste of this. Concepts, memories, feelings, emotions—they fall away like leaves from the trees in autumn. What is left then, or what is released? The unnameable, the incomparable. Beyond words, beyond thinking and perception, there is utter bliss. The experiment could lead to this: in a flash, there is unity.

It remains an experiment, a crude tool. Over the centuries and all over the world, many more subtle means have been developed to sublate the *I*-limitations. Forms of meditation, rituals, forms of yoga, prayer—every single one is a means to enter the Immediate and to detach oneself from the attachments of the old *I*.

Anyone using one of these means embarks on a certain path. While on this path, one often learns to employ one's will (through concentration and doing particular exercises) to create a state in which one can let go of the will. Initially, the *I* is made stronger, it is trained, it learns control and focus. The inner contradictions are sublated. Subsequently, one learns to let everything go, to surrender and dissolve oneself.

In his autobiography, *The Way of the White Clouds,* Lama Anagarika Govinda tells of his voyage to a sage hermit in Tibet. He travels for two weeks through the most mountainous territory of the world. Winter is approaching, and the last stage of his trek is through heavy snow. He has to take shelter in the vicinity of the hermit's cave. He decides to go to bed early, so he can leave at first light. Before he falls asleep, however, something miraculous occurs. We quote Govinda:

I had the sensation that somebody took possession of my consciousness . . . that I had no more control over my thoughts, but that somebody else was thinking them—and that, slowly but surely, I was losing my own identity. And then I realized that it could be none other than the hermit, who, by directing his attention upon me, had entered my body and taken possession of it, probably quite unintentionally, due to the power of his concentration and my own lack of resistance in the moment while I was hovering between the waking and the sleeping state. There was nothing aggressive in his presence—on the contrary.

Govinda recounts that he feels attracted to that other force, and then realizes that this is not just another experience, but that he will merge completely into the other and lose his identity forever if he surrenders now. He is gripped by a deep fear, "the indescribable, inexpressible fear of emptiness—to be blown out like a candle—to fall in the Nameless Void, a void from which there would be no return!"

In a final effort, he gets out of his bed. He lights a candle, and struggling to stay conscious, he takes his shaving mirror, paper, a piece a charcoal, and starts to draw his self-portrait. "No matter that the temperature in the room was below freezing-point—I had to do something and do it quickly!" He succeeds in drawing himself, and as he gets further into his portrait, the foreign force leaves him. When the portrait is done, he is his own self again. He goes to bed and sleeps peacefully till morning.

The next day, he descends into the hermitage and is received very hospitably. Govinda has a fascinating talk with the hermit. During their conversation, the previous night's memories fade away. He is a little ashamed of his deep fear, and he doesn't mention the occurrence. He does ask the hermit to write something in his meditation book, which he always carries with him.

The hermit hesitates for a moment, but then grabs a bamboo pen and fills a page with Tibetan characters.

"There!" he said. "Here is your subject for meditation: *The Eighteen Kinds of Voidness!*" So he was aware of what had happened to me in the previous night and what I had tried to hide! I was deeply moved. And when leaving the Great Hermit, after having received his blessings, I felt that I had not only met him in the flesh but also in the spirit: in a manner which revealed both his spiritual power and his human kindness. . . . I shall never forget the peace of his hermitage amidst the eternal snow and the lessons he taught me: that we cannot face the Great Void before we have the strength and the greatness to fill it with our entire being. Then the void is not the negation merely of our limited personality, but the Plenum-Void which includes, embraces, and nourishes it, like the womb of space in which the light moves eternally without ever being lost.

Nan-in, a Japanese master during the Meiji era (1868–1912), received a university professor who came to inquire about Zen. Nan-in served tea. He poured his visitor's cup full, and then kept on pouring. The professor watched the overflow until he no longer could constrain himself. "It is overfull. No more will go in!"

"Like this cup," Nan-in said, "you are full of your own opinions and speculations. How can I show you Zen unless you first empty your cup?"

PAUL REPS, *ZEN FLESH, ZEN BONES*

The Reversal

We develop our possibilities, we observe discipline, we learn techniques, we become a full-grown personality. And then it turns out that our voyage hasn't ended, because our inner voice isn't satisfied, despite all of this growth. And perhaps the worst thing is that we are still afraid of death, and we allow that fear to determine us. Something different is called for. Letting go. Relinquishing. Detaching. Surrendering.

We take that path. We learn to let go and to surrender. To do that, we learn to meditate and to pray, we learn techniques to liberate ourselves. We do asanas, we sing mantras, we visualize, we learn from the Native Americans or the Aborigines of Australia. But all this learning still takes an effort of the will. It is very positive, one could say; it serves a good cause, but it is still a learning in duality. It doesn't lead to deliverance. For that we need something else. A great leap, as we call it in this book, a turnabout or a reversal.

We have to take that leap or make that reversal ourselves. Nobody does it for us. The fact remains that everything in our lives drives us to the point at which we can turn around. If we don't go to that point willingly, life will make us go there. If we hold ourselves back and resist it, life will demolish and crumble that hold until we stand empty-handed and we have no choice but to go.

Some people are really strong in this sense. They have the ability to make a hold of anything. They are the monarchs who, like king Oedipus, resist life to the bitter end.

In one realm or another, everybody is such a king. No matter how much one is willing, at some point or other everyone holds back. At that very point, life strikes; it rubs and grinds and grates and cuts away until the monarch is forced to recognize the emptiness as reality. Initially, this is a terrible emptiness. The emptiness of loss.

A forty-one-year-old man tells the following:

I had all I wanted: a happy marriage, kids, a nice rewarding job, and a beautiful house. Early one morning in December 1983, we found our one-year-old daughter dead in her crib. SIDS. I never experienced a greater shock— she was a great kid, had never been ill, and was ostensibly quite normal and healthy, without any warning signs— dead, just like that! We had a very difficult time with it. It was terrible. My trust in life was shaken. Death had entered my life in a most brutal way. It dawned on me that everything was possible, even the worst.

At the end of 1984, our son was born. In the beginning of 1985, my wife was diagnosed with an aggressive form of breast cancer. There was no hope for recovery. The ensuing therapies were merely aimed at slowing the process: chemotherapy, radiation treatments every other day. Periods of hope followed periods of despair. We tried to mobilize all forces in the fight against the cancer. We visualized, we prayed. A circle of people around us prayed for us and supported us. I kept working for a long time, took care of my wife, our son, and my wife's son from a previous marriage. On top of that, I did all the household work. When we finally were able to get household help, I was completely exhausted and ended up getting sick myself.

My wife's situation deteriorated by the day. Her breasts were one big festering wound. She was in a lot of pain and, in the end, was lying in a bed in the living room. She couldn't walk anymore. It was really hard to bear. Until the end, she was grieving over the daughter we lost and very sad to have to leave her little son behind. We cried a lot together, prepared for our final good-byes. Then one evening in September 1987 she died, unexpectedly after all.

After my wife's passing away, all that had happened really sunk in: almost all my life's expectations and ideas had fallen to pieces. I had totally lost my footing. I was even being laid off from the school where I taught because of a merger.

It was obvious that I couldn't go on living the "old" way. Characteristic for this period was that the process lasted much, much longer than I had anticipated. At first, I encountered every level of resistance: I fell into a depression, was angry, wanted to kill myself, felt like giving up or going crazy. I couldn't and didn't want to see light anymore. Everything was equally dark and futile, empty. I was unable to imagine a future for myself. I especially felt grief, sadness, and loss. Hadn't I experienced everything life could possibly offer, hadn't I experienced intense happiness and utter despair? What else could come? There was nothing left. I was floating in an empty space, detached from the old, aimed at nothing but survival.

Love changed all of this. I fell in love, and through it, I again encountered all aspects of my desire to repair the "old." I saw how much I wanted to fill the empty space my wife had left, and how impossible that was. I could not replace her, and I wasn't ready yet for a true, new love relationship. I broke up the relationship.

Then I started, very gradually, to accept that I was alone and was living with my children. I had to answer all my questions, one after the other. Each time, I had to choose the things that brought me closer to myself, until finally, nothing was left but reality. At that stage, reality permeated me to my very core: I am living with two children whom I love dearly, I am able to receive life's impulses, and I am starting to give my own answers again. I am starting to shine again. I am longing to express myself, to become myself again more and more.

I am following, although I don't know where I am being led to.

In this process, I received help and guidance from people who stayed close to me, from dreams that made things clear, and from my own creative channel, which enabled me to give shape to what was happening on a level other than language and mental consciousness.

The Desert

"I saw how much I wanted to fill the empty space my wife had left, and how impossible that was." This statement portrays a very dramatic process in straight words. Who doesn't recognize this? Who hasn't tried to fill an irreplaceable emptiness with some surrogate of that which one wished for? And who has had the subsequent courage to admit that the surrogate was fake, and chose not to settle for it? He who chooses the emptiness over the surrogate is, in the language of the myth, a hero. He is who he is.

The hero of this book, Oedipus, has to deal with this temptation also, at the very moment he begins to accept his fate. When things go badly for him, he becomes tempted by resentment, bitterness, a long depression, self-pity, and self-hatred. Everything has been taken away from him. His senses are allowed no satisfaction. He is alone with his painful feelings and torturous thoughts. He can call no place on earth home; no road leads him to a destination to settle down. He has to wander continuously, hoping for a final solution promised him by the god Apollo.

During his wanderings, he finally begins to forgive others and, more important, himself. He lets go of the past and becomes silent. But then, at the very moment he begins to find peace, the past surfaces again. His son Polyneices and his uncle Creon, who had succeeded Oedipus as the king of Thebes, beseech him. Both try to tempt him to take their sides in their conflict and to return to

Thebes. They offer him the fulfillment of his old deepest desires.

Oedipus refuses, however. He sees through the intrigues. Moreover, it is no longer his wish to return and to be honored anew. He doesn't strive for a restoration of his old glory. The only thing he longs for now is deliverance.

Through the ages, the desert has been the symbol of the loneliness and abandonment that human beings experience when they retreat from the lives they know. The desert is wild and desolate— a place of few sensory stimulations. It is the place par excellence for repenting and meditating. This is the place where the initiate who enters the abandonment receives the visions of his future tasks in life.

Members of many Native American tribes go into the desert when they feel that something in their lives has to change or when a fundamental issue arises. With no weapons, no protection, and no food or water, they spend four days in loneliness. They meditate and wait for a vision. This is called a vision quest.

He who enters the desert denies himself everything that could offer fulfillment. Because he doesn't fill himself with anything, space opens up for the other and the unexpected. Some do indeed find new inspiration, a vision. Some do not persevere and, without having found anything, return very depressed—and especially very thirsty. Some do not return. The dangers are real.

You can imagine what it is like to go into the emptiness, leaving everything you own behind but your fears, your ways of thinking, and your opinions. Those you take along. Thoughts of wild animals, fears that you will die of thirst, reminders of what your physician advised you—all those thoughts are brought along. You fill the desert around you with them. You can imagine that, after a while, those thoughts attain such a high degree of truth that you take them absolutely seriously and you allow yourself to be determined by them. You started out full of good intentions, but after four hours you are no longer having fun. A desert is, after all, a desert. Four hours later, you notice that the vultures have come noticeably closer; after another two hours, you realize that this is not for you, and you limp back to civilization. Staying in the desert demands the utmost of you. Only if you wager everything might you get through the eye of the needle.

The spirit immediately drove him out into the wilderness. And he was out in the wilderness forty days, tempted by Satan; and he was with the wild beasts; and the angels ministered to him.

THE GOSPEL ACCORDING TO MARK, 1:12–13

The Temptations

The Native American vision quest lasts four days. Another vision quest, Jesus' vision quest in the wilderness, lasted forty days. This is an important episode in Jesus' life, with which the Gospel according to Mark dealt summarily. Not a word too many! Let us follow the text closely.

After the baptism in the river Jordan (see the initiation phases described in chapter 1), Jesus is immediately led into the desert by the spirit, the free principle. In the English translation the word used is *wilderness;* in the Greek original the word is *eremos,* meaning "forsaken, lonely, wild, uncultivated." The essence, the spirit, leads into forsakenness, and whoever follows the spirit is tested in this state of loneliness.

At the end, it is mentioned that he was there in the midst of "the wild beasts and the angels." When we have arrived in this wilderness, we have the opportunity to live in peace with our drives and our instincts. We don't suppress "the wild beasts" anymore, and we aren't torn apart by them. We are riding "on the back of the tiger," as we described it in chapter 4. All animality rises up in us and is at our disposition. But we can also get in touch directly with "the angels." As soon as we no longer obscure the forces of light, the inspirations and intuitions, with our temporal *I,* they serve us.

The beasts and the angels do not exclude each other, they belong together. On different levels, both are expressions of the single force of love. If we love the high and the low in equal measure, we are rooted in the earthly and we are receptive to the heavenly. The animal ascends and is transformed in the descending light that takes on form.

But before this is completed, there is the temptation to yet again fill the emptiness. The old tempter, the Guardian of the Threshold, tests us to see if we are truly detached from the fruits of time and space.

Other gospels provide more details. The Gospel according to Matthew states: "And he fasted for forty days and forty nights, and afterwards he was hungry" (4:2). Here, we find confirmation that we are not solely dealing with a passive dwelling in the emptiness but, to an equal degree, with an active attitude of fasting. It is an intentional abstinence not only from food and water, but from everything that seems to be rewarding to the personality—the "earthly food": physical sensory stimulations, emotional reactions, mental images. The fasting continues day and night, meaning that even sleep does not affect him, for forty days. Forty, the number of *the full measure.*

Oedipus roams the wilderness of the world these "forty days," when he finally arrives at the holy ground of the Dread Goddesses. It is there that his fate has reached its full measure, and it is there that he is tested one last time by the voices of his past.

The Gospel according to Matthew states that Jesus was hungry in the end—after forty days. This statement is not devoid of humor. The desire-nature speaks. At this point, the adversary appears. Here he is called Satan or the devil, the same one that tried to tempt Gautama under the bodhi tree in the form of Mara.

And the tempter came and said to him, "If you are the son of God, command these stones to become loaves of bread." But he answered, "It is written, 'Man shall not live by bread alone, but by every word that proceeds from the mouth of God.'"

THE GOSPEL ACCORDING TO MATTHEW, 4:3–4

Stones and Bread

Everything you think you need to live as you usually do is absent in the wilderness. You truly do not know what the next moment will bring. You detach from all those insistent desires or the frustration drives you mad.

During this fast, voices come from the inside and the outside: "Don't you have a great creative ability? You could do something fun. You could imagine something or you could do something that might not suit you, but it might at least be nourishing. You can turn stones into loaves of bread. If you lack something, why don't you simply make it?"

Everyone has those highly personal stones that could be turned into bread in the emptiness. They are lifeless objects and lifeless contacts that can be adorned with private pleasures, so it appears as if there is some fun to be had in the emptiness. This is humankind's great negative creative power—the power to build worlds by oneself, worlds that are not connected to the stream of life. This negative force is sometimes called materialism.

Our civilization fears nothing more than the emptiness. We try to avoid, in every way imaginable, being alone with ourselves. Collectively, we fill up the void with gadgets, sound carriers, and image producers. The moment we feel any kind of displeasure, the mouth is offered a taste. We fill life with relationships, and if we feel any lasting discomfort, the doctor prescribes a pill. This is pure materialism: suggestions of the Guardian of the Threshold of possessions.

The answer to these temptations is "Man shall not live by bread alone, but by every word that proceeds from the mouth of God." That is a most radical answer. Life is not at all about getting fed or being satisfied, first and foremost. The criteria is not whether you are physically and emotionally happy, but whether you are connected to the stream of life. Are you living your life? That is what your life is about. It seems very simple but is really very difficult to do after a "fast of forty days," when you are longing for some degree of personal satisfaction.

The text Jesus cites is from the Old Testament (Deuteronomy 8:3). It is a reference to that other voyage through the wilderness, the departure of the Jewish people from Egypt in their search for the Promised Land. The Israelites were not far into their journey when they started to long for the fleshpots of Egypt. They complained, whereupon God said, "Behold, I will rain bread from heaven for you" (Exodus 16:4). That was manna, the bread God dispenses to check the hunger, the "word that proceeds from the mouth of God."

This manna cannot be kept. You can't accumulate it. You have no control over it. It doesn't come at your moment, but in the right moment. Wanting to live on manna demands surrender and trust. If those are lacking, the tempter comes.

Everyone has to deal with this temptation on the path of nascency. The moment you start something new, you enter the tension-filled emptiness that is inherent to the new. Then you encounter the voice that says, "Wouldn't you like a cup of coffee before you start work? Another cup maybe? Do you want something to eat, want to talk, want to buy something?" Anything is better than having to bear the silence and having to endure the loss to the bitter end.

Then the devil took him to the holy city, and set him on the pinnacle of the temple, and he said to him, "If you are the son of God, throw yourself down; for it is written, 'He will give his angels charge of you,' and 'On their hands they will bear you up, lest you strike your foot against a stone.'"

*Jesus said to him, "Again it is written,
'You shall not tempt the Lord, your God.'"*

THE GOSPEL ACCORDING TO MATTHEW, 4:5–7

The Perfect Protection

So goes the seduction of the advanced person. This temptation surfaces once you are aware that life is good and that its meaningfulness is always greater than any negativity. It is the voice that says, "If everything has meaning, you can do anything. There are no restrictions anymore. You can drive as fast as you want, you can take any drug you want on your voyage of discovery, you don't have to think of others. After all, everything is love. Everything will turn out right." Very cunning!

This is a form of spiritual nihilism. It is a high and holy argument, but these beautiful arguments only provide a license not to have to limit one's personal needs. It is nothing but narcissism with a holy sauce.

Several contemporary spiritual movements profess to this train of thought. "Follow your impulses," they say, "don't differentiate, do whatever you feel like." It is indeed amazing to see how great the protection is that life offers, and how much is taken in, ironed out, and comforted. But letting one's personal proclivities grow rampant does not lead to unity. It is a detour. The *I* is turned into a large inflated ball that imagines itself a god or guru, but doesn't serve life.

Jesus says to this temptation of false love, "Again it is written, 'You shall not tempt the Lord, your God.'" Here too he cites a text from the Old Testament (Deuteronomy 6:16), and this quotation also refers to the voyage through the wilderness of the Jewish people.

The people were complaining again, this time about lack of water. The people said, "Is God in our midst or not?" They put God to the test. They demanded that God prove that God was there by saving them and giving them water—a child's demand. Then God said to Moses that he would stand before him on a rock and that Moses should strike the rock with his rod. Moses did so, and water streamed forth from the rock.

Here stones aren't turned into bread, but water comes from stone. Where we, as the people in the wilderness, see only dead matter, God shows us through our guiding principle (Moses) that living water is streaming behind and through the phenomena. Wherever we see God on the rock, living water streams forth from dead matter. That is a potentiality. It is not, however, something self-evident; it is not some sort of "deal"—it is grace.

In his answer to the tempter, Jesus acknowledges that he does not want to command a miracle. He doesn't want to force the issue. His will is enclosed within the Great Will.

Again, the devil took him to a very high mountain, and showed him all the kingdoms of the world and the glory of them; and he said to him, "All these I will give you, if you will fall down and worship me." Then Jesus said to him, "Be gone, Satan! for it is written, 'You shall worship the lord your God and him only shall you serve.'"

THE GOSPEL ACCORDING TO MATTHEW, 4:8–10

Power over the World

The temptation of power is the most powerful bait ever, and the hook hidden inside has the most barbs. Everyone, even the most noble people, will have to fight this temptation.

If you had total power, you could fix anything! After all, the misery of the world is the result of obstruction, delays, and petty selfishness. You could get rid of those with one stroke of your pen and the world would be saved. There would be no more discrimination and no more concentration camps, the destruction of nature would be halted, wealth would be redistributed fairly, and so on. The world would become utopia.

But my utopia isn't yours. And supposing I am the one in power, I force my ideals on you. While I seemingly achieve the good, communication is made impossible, because true communication only exists where no power is exerted. By letting the good happen, I suppress the other wishes outside of me, and I suppress that which is unfinished within myself. In this way, the negative drives within me increase their hold on me and, through me, on the world as a whole. I turn into a tyrant, a tyrant with high ideals who strives for the best. No doubt, this is the case for all tyrants.

The only thing you have to do to achieve this power is to bow before that deepest voice of your own negativity. This means that you don't face your negativity, that you don't recognize it as a real problem, but that you turn away from it and, therefore, allow it to take control of you. You are kneeling before the evil and, parallel to it, you are kneeling before the external form.

Great spirits fall for this. This is the third temptation that comes after the first two. It is not the most faint of heart that are tempted by this. One bows very intelligently and intentionally and even a little bit melancholically before something one actually doesn't desire, because, so the argument goes, one is realistic and wants to achieve the highest possible.

This is such a generally accepted practice that those in power who think and act in this manner are held in high esteem, while everybody knows, deep down, that they sold their souls to the devil. We disdain their cunning and their ability to make the bad appear good, but we don't condemn it openly because they are only doing on a large scale what we ourselves do on a small scale. We are accomplices.

You can reason with this temptation, but if that is the only thing you do, you remain caught up in it. If you want to free yourself of this Guardian of the Threshold, you should first state unequivocally, "Go away! I will absolutely not go along with you." Only after you have made that choice can you venture an explanation.

The explanation Jesus offers is again derived from the Old Testament (Deuteronomy 6:13). Note that Jesus answers the temptation every time by citing a scriptural text. It is as if he wants to show that these temptations are far from modern or unique. They are of all times, and sagacious people formulated the answers thousands of years ago. Evil isn't revolutionary; it is the same, time and again.

And here, too, the answer is of the greatest simplicity: "You shall worship the lord your God and him only shall you serve." All drive for power, however altruistic it might appear to be, is egotistical. You can only remain free of this last temptation by not aiming at your personal interests and by not pretending that your personal vision is the ultimate truth. This means that you are actively receptive to the One, the Nameless. Here it is called God, elsewhere Tao or Love or Emptiness. "Then the devil left him."

Immediately after this, Jesus gathered a circle of disciples around him and started to preach, to teach, and to heal. Only after he had given his answer to the three temptations was he ready to gather disciples around him and to begin his life's work. Only then could he become a guru and, in full consciousness, help others to leave behind "the fleshpots of Egypt," to go into the "wilderness," to fast there, to experience the loss, to resist temptation, and so to find the path to the "Promised Land," the Full Emptiness.

The Words

In the emptiness, in the wilderness, you can choose to spin illusionary yarns. You can cling to them and build on them. One of these illusions is the illusion of the self-created god and the self-created demon. The first you endow with the highest, the latter with the lowest. You think that you know them and that you can name them.

This is lunacy. God, the word *god,* is a name; it is a label. You can know a label. It is logical to you, because you stuck it on there yourself. What you stuck it on, you can't know. Here we call it the Nameless and the Emptiness. Again, a name.

On the other hand, you can also live in the ongoing experience of emptiness. You can experience that as love. You can also experience that there is guidance in it, that all is as it is. From this experience, you can speak, but not because you are God's beloved emissary. In the wilderness, you are nothing of God. You are abandoned by God and all people. That is the experience one has to know in order to speak based in God.

Chuang Tzu phrases it as follows (Book 26):

> The fish trap exists because of the fish; once you've gotten the fish, you can forget the trap. The rabbit snare exists because of the rabbit; once you've gotten the rabbit, you can forget the snare. Words exist because of meaning; once you've gotten the meaning, you can forget the words. Where can I find a man who has forgotten words so I can have a word with him?

And so it is: if man desires that a new creation come out of him, then he must come with all his potentiality to the state of nothing, and then God brings forth in him a new creation, and he is like a fountain that does not run dry and a stream that does not become exhausted.

MARTIN BUBER, *THE LEGEND OF THE BAAL-SHEM*

The Last Steps

Back to Oedipus. His story is almost at an end. He has arrived at his destination, the sacred grounds of the Dread Goddesses. They are described as the "daughters of Earth and Darkness." Later in the tragedy they are called, oddly enough, the "All-Seeing Kindly Ones."

The Dread Goddesses pursue criminals without granting them any rest and drive them to madness in the end. They look horrible: the hair on their heads consists of snakes and they wave torches around in the dark of night. They are the expression of the guilt that possesses everyone who acted against the laws of life. Oedipus is driven along by them. That is why he can't find any rest.

He cannot rest until he stops fighting and, as it were, no longer places his feelings of guilt outside of himself. Then he can say: "This is who I was; I am not like that anymore. I am no longer guilty, because I don't act like that anymore, I don't think like that anymore, and I don't feel like that anymore." Then the guilt is wiped out and he is able to arrive at the sacred place. The "Wrathful Ones" have become the "Kindly Ones," as all feelings of guilt truly lived through are turned into thankfulness. The medicine was bitter, but it did heal.

Here, on this spot, Oedipus is called. A thunderstorm comes up. Thunderclap follows upon thunderclap. Oedipus says, "Now it is time to go. The hand of God directs me." And a little further, "Hermes is leading me, and the Queen of the Netherworld." They lead him into the mystery: Hermes who connects the high and the low, this world and the other world; Hermes, the initiator, sometimes called the Conductor of Souls. And with him is Persephone, the daughter of Demeter and, at the same time, Demeter herself. Demeter is the Great Mother, about whom we wrote in the first chapter. Their presence indicates that Oedipus is now reconciled with the father and the mother, with man and woman. His trials have ended.

They are the last visible divine figures who can be named. After this, the mystery comes. There is "a Voice . . . a terrifying voice. A god is calling, 'Oedipus! Oedipus!' it cried, again and again. 'It is time: you stay too long.'"

Theseus, Oedipus's friend, accompanies him a little distance. But for Theseus, too, there is a point he cannot go beyond. "The

King was standing alone holding his hand before his eyes as if he had seen some terrible sight that no one could bear to look upon." Oedipus enters the Indescribable. "Certain it is that he was taken without a pang, without grief or agony." Where he goes is not told. He is taken up in the mystery, and "this is the end of tears."

Oedipus has left his Egypt. He has wandered through the wilderness the full "forty years." He did not give in to temptations. Now he has entered the Promised Land. We, as writers or readers, can't follow him there. His story has come to an end.

Unphased Phases

The Oedipus myth deals with *the one initiation* a human being can go through. Nothing is said about the phases of the path of initiation. You could also say that Oedipus advances through all stages at once. When he sleeps, he keeps everything in, and when he awakens, he lets everything go. There are no four phases—there is one leap.

This holds true from a particular point of view. A valley looks very different from the top of the mountain than it does when one walks through it. The Oedipus myth is told from the top of the mountain. It is the story of a hero—not a person, but the archetypal human being.

Down below in the valley, people are walking. They look up at the mountain. Once they have arrived at the top, they undoubtedly will also see that the various paths form one road; from below, however, there seem to be many paths with many possible choices and a number of clear markings. That is a reality too.

The next chapter is about this reality. There we will take a closer look, independent of the Oedipus myth, at the path of initiation as a path of phases taken in leaps.

ten

Phases of Initiation

A pure uniqueness and a pure perfection are one, and he who has become so entirely individual that no otherness any longer has power over him or place in him has completed the journey and is redeemed and rests in God. "Every man shall know and consider that in his qualities he is unique in the world and that none like him ever lived, for had there ever been before some one like him, then he would not have needed to exist."

MARTIN BUBER, *THE LEGEND OF THE BAAL-SHEM*

You are a new manifestation of life. There is no other meaning than for you to become who you are. When you achieve that, you fulfill yourself, and only in this way do you fulfill the meaning of your life for the larger whole.

Thus the central question is, Who are you? And it is certain that the answer to the question can be found only within yourself. Yet, for a large part of your life, you are engaged in finding the answer outside of yourself. Apparently, there are other forces at work.

In the previous chapter, we have described those forces and

commented on them. We saw that they are part of the road that eventually merges with the emptiness. No part of this road can be skipped. Your experiences on this road, in search for answers outside yourself, can lead to the search for the answer within yourself.

Once you have reached this stage, the path of your life has become the path of initiation.

Desires and Pain

Before you arrive at the point at which you turn inward voluntarily, you can't really speak of true wishes or desires. You are not allowing your real wishes to permeate you. You experience as normal the large difference between how you would really like to lead your life and the reality of your existence. "That's life," you tell yourself.

Sometimes the difference gets to be too much, and suddenly you feel the pang caused by the gap between your true desires and your everyday reality. But you regard that reality as something outside of you, as something you will have to learn to live with. So your only recourse is to suppress the pain. You quickly think of something else. You ignore the pain, and you avoid situations that remind you how unhappy you really are. People around you also consider it normal that you do this. "You aren't seeking out trouble, are you?" they ask.

You don't think too much about what you really want, you don't ask yourself what you would change in your life, and you take care not to touch the "electric fence" marking the boundaries of your life. Those are the laws you live by on the road of growth, the road of rising, shining, and declining.

Yet, your desires keep gnawing at you; they keep forcing themselves on you. You collide with your boundaries, and you begin to see those boundaries less and less as something that is a part of life, and more and more as something you have created yourself. You start to pay attention to the things you truly want. Pain is not something to be avoided at all costs anymore. The path of initiation begins.

On the path of initiation, you begin to take your deepest desires seriously, and you want to make them come true. You view these deepest desires—your wishes—as real. They bring to light how loving you are and how many opportunities your true nature offers you. In other words, within your deepest desires, you know a world of which you are the core creator. Your ideals do not come from outside of you; they don't just come out of nowhere. They are made of the same raw material you are made of.

The important thing now is to make your dearest wish your reality. The rest, ordinary reality, you now call illusion. Pain is the difference between that which you know in your desires and the so-called real world.

Now that you are no longer dependent on outside influences, you are permanently engaged in dissolving pain. You don't avoid the tension of the undesirable anymore. You know when something doesn't really suit you or when something angers you. You know now that your surroundings are all around you, and all the lovelessness around you becomes a matter of personal concern. Only you can solve what is happening in your world.

The Way Home

The path of initiation is not just a path of suffering. It is not just about pain. You become receptive to everything you didn't want to know before, when it was too risky to know. Your senses open up, your outer as well as your inner eyes and ears. You meet people who speak the language of your heart and who join you. You get in touch with your inner voice. You experience that your inner voice, just like your outer friends, is not a "know-it-all" who prescribes how you should behave. There is nothing outside of you that knows who you really are and what you ought to do. In essence, your inner voice is the voice of your deepest wishes.

You discover these wishes gradually, because it takes a while for you to get used to the thought that you create the world around you from your inside. You are still learning to detach yourself from the outside and not think of yourself as dependent on it.

You are less and less a derivative of the outside, but during this process of liberation, the term *outside* takes on a deeper meaning. Initially, *outside* was the concrete outside world. But now, *outside* gradually becomes the things inside of you that you identify with but that are not you. Only now do you notice how much of the outside you have absorbed and how much, in the words of Martin Buber, belongs to the other that has power over you. Even if you are completely alone, the outside is still in you. And the more you detach yourself from it, the more you get in touch with the desire to be your true self.

You are like a seed. The seed has within it all knowledge of what it will grow into. It is known, but as yet a secret in time and space. Wanting to know what it will grow into leads nowhere. The secret reveals itself when the seed yields to the movement coming from the core, the movement of the desire to make itself known in time and space. Your deepest wish is the core of who you are. It indicates, very precisely, what you have to do to develop in fullness. It is a wise teacher that never demands of you what you cannot do. The longing shows you the way home.

Phases of Initiation—The Path

The path of unification with yourself is a journey through various worlds. Every world is its own reality, with corresponding wishes, behaviors, experiences, guardians, and nightmares. You dwell in each world until you have traveled through it completely. You have taken up everything of that world into your consciousness. It is available to you. You begin to long for the next world. At each new stage of your journey, you are more awake, more light, more concrete, more loving, more creative, and more free than you were before.

These stages are the phases of initiation we described in chapter 1. We repeat them here schematically.

First Initiation:

Birth   The transition from the trial path to the path of initiation.

CHARACTERISTIC: Form crisis.

TO BE LEARNED: To subject the physical body and one's actions in the physical world to the higher principle, the soul.

The personality is no longer in charge, but serves.

KEY WORDS: Discipline, attunement, detachment.

ELEMENT: Earth.

CHAKRAS: Link between solar plexus and heart.

Second Initiation:

Baptism   CHARACTERISTIC: Emotional crisis.

TO BE LEARNED: To control the emotional body by cleansing the emotions and uniting them with the central source of love.

The astral body functions as a mirror that reflects the soul to the plane of physical experience, without distortions or appropriations.

KEY WORDS: Love, freedom (not suppressing or repressing emotions and not being carried away by emotions).

ELEMENT: Water.

CHAKRAS: Link between sex and throat.

Third Initiation:

Transfiguration CHARACTERISTIC: Mental crisis.

TO BE LEARNED: To give up negative dependency, to know what you think and think what you know.

Thoughts and wishes create new realities. One actively participates in creation by being a cocreator.

The personality in its three articulations (physical, astral, and mental) is now a single harmonious and serving instrument.

KEY WORDS: Bring into the light and create freely.

ELEMENT: Air.

CHAKRAS: Link between forehead and crown.

Fourth Initiation:

Crucifixion CHARACTERISTIC: "Dark night of the soul."

TO BE LEARNED: The soul isn't entitled to an independent existence, either.

The soul burns with the personality and becomes potential again that can assume any form (the Phoenix).

KEY WORDS: Surrender, death, rebirth, not my vision but the Great Will.

ELEMENT: Fire.

CHAKRAS: Link between root and crown.

These four initiations—and particularly the first three—happen in all realms of existence. The shock waves that accompany a transition undermine all certainties. And once we have made the transition, we are a noticeably different person. There are concrete differences in concrete realms, such as the relationship to one's parents, sickness and death, sex and love, money, possessions, and power, to name just a few of the more important ones.

Phases of Initiation—The Guardians

In front of the gate leading into a next world is always a guardian, and as with every guardian, passing by will be a close shave.

On the path of unfolding your unlimited potential, your parents (and, in a larger sense, your authorities, your teachers, the people you look up to) are the guardians that want to hold you down and restrict you. They demand (or you assume that they demand) that you become as they are, as if you can thereby offer them the guarantee that they did a good job. They can (or you assume that they can) stop you from freely discovering that you are carrying your source of love inside of you and that you can only find your own form if you keep going back to that source of love.

You could stand nailed to the ground for a long time searching for the right answer or waiting for your parents to change. In that case, you aren't seeing your parents, you're merely seeing yourself. You could pretend to go on, outwitting your parents. Then you aren't seeing your parents, either—you are pretending that you don't have them in you.

Oedipus did that. He pretended to go on, he pretended to detach himself from the past. He turned off a part of his mind. But he didn't turn off the guardians; they gathered together and waited, as guardians should, until he had reached the full measure of his power and had gained the greatest esteem possible. At that point, unexpectedly, his people were hit by disasters, and he didn't know what to do. His people's fate touched him so greatly that he asked for help. He didn't ask the oracle to bring an end to the disasters; he asked to know the cause of their suffering. He admitted that he didn't know the cause and that he, with all his power, didn't have a solution. He really wanted to know the truth. That was the step he took—the step that put him on the threshold of no-man's-land in the name of a higher truth. Then all the guardians came forward.

Nothing was forgotten. He had to let everything get to him simultaneously. Only when he did that did he leave his parents and become truly alone.

As we saw in chapter 6, the three basic drives in the life of the human personality are sexuality, power, and possessions. Every human being has to find a relationship to these. What distinguishes humans from animals is that humans can choose how they are going to deal with their instincts. During a lifetime, a person can change from being a member of the herd, pushed on by others, to an individual living consciously. Because of his consciousness, a human is able to direct his animal instincts as wisely as possible, while preserving all their inherent powers and energies. It all depends on what he wants to use them for.

Saving himself and keeping his family together is the least a person can choose. In that case, he will be governed by sexuality, power, and possessions. He develops an understanding for animals, so that he and his surroundings can master them to the best of their abilities within the norms of society.

Only when his interests go beyond his own and his family's boundaries will he wonder what he is maximally capable of. The more he views the interests of the whole of humanity as his own interests, the more all-encompassing his vision becomes and the better he wants to and is able to direct his instincts. He will regard all that lives and exists on earth as his family, and he will attune all his actions to the common good.

Then he has taken the animal within himself by the hand and linked it to the highest goal. With all his heart, he unites himself with everything around him (sexuality), he shines his light on the largest circle possible (power), and he passes on to the world what he receives of life (property).

Transition and Progress

Life does not consist of initiations and guardians alone. After one passes a certain guardian, an initiation follows. That is a leap; a new world is set free. Life as such is bathed in a new light, and everything that until then seemed "logical" and "normal" falls apart and takes on a new form. Everything has to be renamed. This takes time, patience, and love.

The period right after an initiation is taken up with scouting out the new land and making it inhabitable. It is a period of growth that can last many years. Only after large tracts of the land are known, after one has experienced everything there is to experience and learned everything there is to be learned, does the next guardian loom at the horizon. The shock waves set in again. The next initiation can take place.

In this chapter, we will try to describe the initiation stages in terms of a number of concrete themes, namely parents, sexuality, power, and possessions. First, we will investigate how each phase expresses itself in one's relationship to one's parents. After that, we will discuss how the initiation stages can be detected in the realms of sexuality, power, and possessions.

We will begin each topic with a description of the "old trusty world" (Phase 0). Then we'll proceed to a description of the trial path, the first guardian that appears, and the first initiation (Phase 1). We will continue until we have reached the third guardian and the third initiation. For the fourth initiation and beyond, one can no longer speak of specific relations to parents, sexuality, possessions, and power. The fourth initiation and beyond will not be dealt with in this book.

For a detailed and systematic overview of the phases, we refer to the chart at the end of the book.

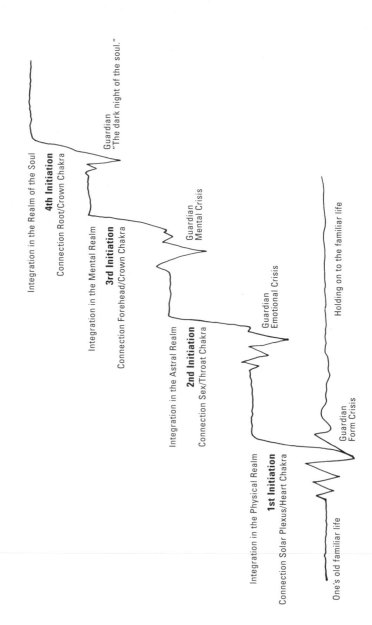

The Initiation Mountain Range

Integration in the Realm of the Soul
4th Initiation
Connection Root/Crown Chakra

Guardian
"The dark night of the soul."

Integration in the Mental Realm
3rd Initiation
Connection Forehead/Crown Chakra

Guardian
Mental Crisis

Integration in the Astral Realm
2nd Initiation
Connection Sex/Throat Chakra

Guardian
Emotional Crisis

Integration in the Physical Realm
1st Initiation
Connection Solar Plexus/Heart Chakra

Guardian
Form Crisis

Holding on to the familiar life

One's old familiar life

The Parents on the Path of Initiation

You literally come from your parents. They are the foundation of your life on earth. You came forth from these two people, each with their own but also complementary characteristics. Through nature and nurture, you have absorbed these characteristics, but you are more. You are also somebody different, not simply your parents' offspring; you are a stranger that exists in his own right.

The consciousness development that you go through takes place parallel to the development that your relationship to your parents goes through. As mentioned earlier, it is important in this respect to realize that your parents are a symbol for all people that you look up to in life.

Phase 0:
My Parents Are There for Me

For a long time, you as a human being do not want to know who your father and your mother are. You also do not want to know who you are. Your father and mother are there for you. You still have to become somebody.

For as long as you are a child, you are right to think that your parents are there to help you grow. But when your body, your emotions, and your faculty of judgment are fully grown, you are given a choice: are you going to remain your parents' child or will you mature and assume your own identity?

You can stay where you are and remain dependent on your parents. In that case, you are not using your will to become a free and independent personality. You follow the path of least resistance—you follow in the footsteps of your father and mother.

Phase 1:
I Distance Myself from My Parents in the Name of Freedom

The trial path begins as soon as you move to find out who you are, independent of your parents. Then, for the first time in your life, the Guardian of the Threshold enters your life. He is reflected in your parents who say, *"Don't do this to us, don't behave so differently from us. Don't we belong together? Nobody knows better than we what you need, child!"*

If your parents really try to stop you, you will have to distance yourself from them, literally, in order to proceed on your path. You regard your freedom as more important than the pain you cause your parents. For a while, you think it is their fault that you aren't free. You think that you will gain freedom by negating them—by doing the opposite of what they have taught you. The ties between you and them are so deep that you lose yourself again in their absence. Again and again, you require distance to find yourself. It appears as if they don't want to understand what this is all about, and that is why they keep tying you down.

But then you begin to experience that your tendency to fit in is deeper than you thought it was. You notice how much of your parents' thoughts and feelings you have absorbed. You realize that you are fighting yourself. Outside is not outside, it is inside! For the first time, you truly begin to wonder what your shortcomings are, what is holding you back from being yourself. You begin to listen to criticism.

In this undertaking, you are primarily self-directed. And even though you are freer in your relationship with your parents and don't condemn them as much anymore, they do have to appreciate what you are doing, and most of the time, they won't. You still regard yourself as special—the center of the world. But you are truly searching.

This self-directedness changes when you begin to wonder what the *purpose* of all of this is. What is the purpose of your life? What do you really have to offer? At this stage, you are no longer primarily directed toward the question, How can I please myself and keep it that way?

The resistance you felt against life dissolves. You take an interest in the essence of the other and, hence, in the essence of your parents. You regard life as a road on which everything you go through aids you in becoming yourself again. Here, the first initiation announces itself: "I exist, independent of my thoughts, my emotions, and my body. On the inside, I am eternal and untouchable. I experience an energetic contact with the stream of life. I want to follow that stream from within. I know that nothing in the world can stop me from becoming who I am. I have nothing to lose but what I am not."

Now, the next guardian rises up. Your parents act it out as follows, *"You're wrong. Nobody is absolutely good. We're all sinners. Everybody has shortcomings. If we want to have meaning for another, we'll have to learn not to think of ourselves first. You can't have everything you want."*

Phase 2:
I Want to Show Myself to My Parents

If you do not allow this voice to hold you back, you will have to rely on yourself from now on. You leave behind the beliefs and the philosophy of your parents. You know that you are the creator of your own life, and you want to learn to take responsibility for it, 100 percent. Ahead of you is the task to align your thoughts, emotions, and actions with this inner knowledge.

The word *giving* is starting to gain meaning. Giving does not mean performing a task for another anymore. You give when you reveal yourself in your relation to the other. Then, you become who you are. That person hasn't been created yet—that is why you have something to give.

To begin with, at this stage, you have to deal with your emotions, with your personality that does and does not want to learn to surrender itself. Your personality behaves as it used to, as if you had to make sure that you get what you need. The emotions act up. They won't give up. They don't really "know" that there is a deeper self that is taking over. When they notice it, they'll really act up initially. Time and again, you will be swept along. Hence, your parents (and your surroundings) won't notice much of your new belief. They see a struggle, difficulties, pain, and, besides that, a kind of stubborn persistence in something that is as yet invisible to them. Neither are you successful in articulating your newly found insights in a clear and evenhanded manner. Your inner certainty hasn't become flesh and blood sufficiently.

It is difficult to turn into deeds the inner certainty that you are good. Can you really trust your heart? Will you ever be a spontaneously loving person, even when it is difficult? The guardian that shows up here will of course tell you that it is impossible. *Your parents simply represent this guardian by being who they are, with all their shortcomings. In your experience, it requires a superhuman effort to keep originating from within yourself in the relationship with them.* Before you know it, you are reacting again and closing off your heart. They confront you very directly with the question of whether you can originate from yourself, everywhere and all the time.

Yet you know that you can be and want to be permanently loving. You continue on your path. Gradually, you notice that you can get the upper hand over your negativity. Your love appears to be stronger than your emotions. You learn to get in touch with others from within your very self. You give in to your desire for intimacy. A feeling of tenderness is set free inside of you. Love begins to flow. You begin to be humble and to care for people around you spontaneously. The deep fear of falling, if you were to give up control over yourself and the other, dissipates. You venture with increasing pleasure into the unknown. You can trust your feelings. It becomes peaceful in your life.

You view your parents with different eyes, from the heart. From within yourself, you develop an interest in them, and you want to show them who you are. For the first time, you pay your respects as a completely different person than the bossy child you used to be. Now they begin to see that you are well. They can see it, because it is possible for you to be you, to be at home, with them. They want this because of the true connectedness they have with you.

In this phase, you learn to have control of your feelings instead of being led by your feelings. You learn the language of the heart.

Phase 3:
I Give My Parents Back to Themselves

When you act in the name of love, the inner divisiveness ends. You hand over control of the course of events. You are who you are, completely. Then the veil of wanting to know it all is lifted and your head becomes crystal clear. You are coming home to yourself. You are in unison with the knowledge of the soul. The soul does not think backward or forward, the soul *is*. The thoughts that spring from the soul are simple, close to home, and to the point.

You are standing at the threshold of the next phase, at the threshold of the third initiation. The desire to be permanently free and creative comes to the fore. You are becoming a builder. You know that reality is light and simple, and you want to attune your concrete thinking to it. You want to shine your light in your surroundings. The difficulty here is to keep your head empty, not to feed the thoughts that want to secure the future, but to let go of them.

When you are directing yourself to that, the next guardian takes shape. It says, *"Are you sure? You have to continue what already exists, otherwise things will go wrong. When you start from nothing, there is only a fifty-fifty chance that you will succeed. Yes, feelings might well up in you spontaneously, but thoughts? No. And how do you know whatever pops up by itself is right? No, once you have a thought, you shouldn't let go of it. Where are you going to go in this emptiness? Who is going to show you the way?"* This guardian shows itself in the disguise of your parents by revealing to you the blueprint of the family: *"We are proud of all that you've achieved; you are continuing our work. In this, you honor us. When you continue like that, we can grow old peacefully. Our wishes come true in you."*

You pass this guardian if you are willing to sacrifice everything you derive certainty from and to do nothing but what is dearest to you. You don't commit yourself anymore. You want to be in the here and now in your thinking, and you want to go where your inner voice leads you. After all, you want to play your own music. You are the point of origin in everything you do, completely new.

This is how you change your anchoring point from your personality to your soul. You are learning that not knowing it all is the same as being in touch with everything that is. You are a simple person. People become light in your presence.

You let go of your parents. You see them in their true dimensions. Just like you, they have unlimited possibilities. They relate to their everlasting essence. The parents you used to know are a mere temporary manifestation. They accompanied you for a little while on your path—they provided you with your present shell and they helped you to grow up. By being born from them and by being their child, you have helped them to learn to love unselfishly. You cannot influence their light; at the most, you can converge with it for a moment.

Sexuality—The Light Entering the Lust

One could say that sexuality is an impulse originating from the pelvis that serves to unite you bodily and to experience the height of bodily pleasure. Because of the great power with which sexual energy works within us and because of the great pleasure it brings us, humankind procreates. In a naturally living person, the sexual feeling is always present. It is a fundamental feeling of pleasure and of the joy of living. But, because our society forbids the public display of sexual desires, many people do their utmost to keep these feelings within the boundaries of their skins and to make sure they don't show on their faces.

Phase 0:
Living in Your Head

As soon as you develop an interest in sexuality as a child, there is already a Guardian of the Threshold that says, *"It is better to keep this a secret. People don't like that. Let me live in your head, in the head office, and there I will guard you well."* That is how the light is turned off in your head and sexuality becomes an experience in darkness. This is the end of the period of innocent play. One of the unpleasant side effects of this is that, at the most inopportune moments, your thoughts are occupied with sexual fantasies that cannot be lived out.

For as long as you identify with your personality and are tied to your body, you experience sexuality as an urge that demands release. A tension builds up that can only be lessened in one way, by finding a release. Then the excitement is gone and "normalcy" returns.

Phase 1:
The Child Is Allowed to Play Again

If, at the start of the trial path, the curiosity for who you truly are, independent of your body and your bodily sensations, is awakened, you begin to experience how little life you allow to enter your body. You aren't living in your pelvis anymore. You realize that you are dependent on somebody else to summon your sexual feelings within you. You want the vitality and playfulness of your childhood back, you experience the pain of being closed off from your sexuality, and you begin to take root in the earth. In this manner, you make the stream flow again. Your joy for living awakens.

Here, you are confronted by the old guardian again. It gathers all its strength and says, *"I warned you. What do you want with that flow? If you want to be somebody in this world, you should never let go. You should always think before you do."*

You pass this guardian when it is more important to you to stay alive than to leave a good impression. From a girl, you turn into a woman, from a boy into a man. You develop a personal aura, and you are not attracted to the other's outside but to the energetic emanation coming from him or her. You are directed at a sexual relation that you can enjoy in freedom.

Phase 2:
The Play Becomes Tender

Every time you relinquish control and follow the direction that the flow inspires you to, you feel at home. You know that life is good. In this manner, you can begin to experience that your soul manifests itself within you as an ascending feeling of vital energy. The blessing is coming from below. You want to learn to give yourself to this flow, without any reservations. You want the dotted line to become solid. You are standing in front of the second initiation.

Yet there is the guardian who says, *"You are not going to surrender to something you don't know, are you? You don't know the things within you! And what are you going to do with all that longing? If you release that, it will become much too strong. It will never be satisfied. Why don't you keep a lid on it?"*

You go on. You begin to notice that you are more than your sexual feelings. Being free becomes something different from doing what you feel like. You are learning to contain the sexual energy within your heart. While together with another, the intimacy of the contact is giving you at least as much pleasure as the satisfying of your sexual urges. Following the flow is being prepared, in your heart, to completely lay yourself bare. Even the fear of surrendering is a feeling you can share. The deeply rooted tendency to tie the other to you or, conversely, to cling to your fear slowly dissolves, and in this process, the desire to reveal yourself in all your tenderness is released.

For a long time you thought that you would find fulfillment when somebody else gave you all the love you desired so much. But now that the fire from below is united with the tenderness of your heart, your deepest wish is transformed. To be that "other beloved" yourself, to make your hidden string resonate for the other—that is your desire. All the assumed certainty a love relationship can offer disappears. Loving is the same as wanting to keep leaping into the unknown.

Phase 3:
Light and Pleasure Become One

If you follow the stream of life without constantly looking at yourself, you begin to see yourself and the other with your inner eye. Your ideas dissolve. The sexual stream flows into your head, and there it becomes light.

You begin to focus your attention on the light. Just as the feeling of the stream of life was your guide earlier, now the light in your head becomes the guide. The life inside your pelvis and the warmth of your heart have become a permanent fundamental feeling. This feeling offers you the opportunity to be in the here and now with your thoughts also. At this stage, the next leap announces itself: the leap into the deep of emptiness.

You want to hand yourself over completely to the larger knowledge. The litmus test is whether you are prepared to let go of any thought that goes beyond the here and now, in any situation and with any person.

You begin to feel with your head, instead of using it as a machine of thought. You notice that it is your head that loves the light most. You want to keep your head clear while you are making love. Only now do you notice how the flow of sexuality brings everything to light that you still wanted to hold on to. Anything not related to the moment, the smallest thought, every grain of fantasy, hinders the unification. You want to do everything in your power to let go of that last hold.

At that moment, the next guardian appears. *Its residence is your own head! It is no one but the father of your old thoughts that have become so much a part of you that you forgot you created them yourself. Precisely by just being there, always, it is suggesting that nothing will remain when it leaves. It tells you that it can guarantee the continuity of your being by constantly filling you with food for thought aimed at the future. It will never disappear by itself.*

This guardian is silenced when you love the emptiness more than any experience. Now you have become of this earth, completely; you are here with your pelvis, your heart, and your head. You live in the emptiness. This is how you fulfill the emptiness. You have no need for additional experiences. Knowing and wishing have come together.

Now, you long to rise up spontaneously, wholly new. You wish to offer everything that you call *I* to the unnameable that you cannot know with that *I*. If you come together with your lover in this way, sexuality will give its greatest treasure: the greatest possible lust occurs simultaneously with the greatest possible consciousness. Pleasure and light have become one.

Power—The World Is My Palace of Light

One can deduce the power of the animal from its place in the hierarchy of the animal kingdom and from the size of its territory. How many animals are in the group you lead and how large is your territory? The more power available—the more power and influence you have—the better the chance that you grow old and that your group does well.

The feeling of power is situated in our solar plexus. Because of our instinct of power, we can fend for ourselves. We can make our *I*—and with it our territory—as big as possible. We can have anything we desire. We can fight and win. We can subject the outside world to our will. We can also subject everything inside of us to our will. Everything that exists, we can use as an instrument of the will.

Phase 0:
I Have the Power because Nobody Knows Who I Am

In our society, you are never really open. You can never trust somebody else! So you have to be on guard. You are strong if you are in control and invulnerable; you are weak if you don't know that and show vulnerability.

In your childhood, you develop a defensive mechanism against life. You learn to arm yourself. The more impenetrable your armor, the stronger you feel. Because everybody can meddle with you, you restrict yourself to a very small territory. You withdraw inside yourself, where nobody can find you. At least there, you are free. There, you can imagine a world in which you are the king or queen and where everybody empathizes with you. In the meantime, you make sure that outwardly you resemble the others.

Phase 1:
What Is That Secret of Contact?

As long as you say *I* to that exterior that is visible to others, you have to keep defending yourself. Losing face is losing yourself. You aim for the weaknesses of the people around you; that is how you manipulate them. In chakra terms, you are operating from your solar plexus. You are scared and you threaten. It works; people keep a distance. Secretly, you enjoy the victory you won, but outwardly, you behave nicely. Nobody is allowed to know to what degree you are in charge. You would fall from grace, and that is the last thing you want. Make sure that the outside and the inside are separate!

Sooner or later, a moment will come when you begin to suffer from the fact that you keep everything so tightly under control. This often happens when love enters your life. You are touched inside. Now, the power turns against you. You notice how tense and unnatural you are, how much you are locked up inside yourself. You begin to see how much you exert yourself in pretending to be somebody other than who you are. The trial path begins.

You admit to yourself that you are vulnerable and dependent on the opinion of others. You very much want to be liked for who you are, instead of being regarded as an impressive persona. You want to know the secret of getting in touch.

The guardian that rises up at this moment wants to prevent that. It says, *"Don't give in to that weakness. Do you want to live a boring life, with sweet whisperings and that 'I really need you' stuff? So you are like everybody else, after all? No more fun, that's the end of the game."*

But you continue to follow the thread of your real needs. Your feelings are not an undesirable weakness anymore, they are a sign of inner life. You are interested in your own self and you begin to develop an inner strength. You can relativize.

But you still have the fear of not knowing the effect you have on others. You are still trying to make a good impression, but you are also realizing that that is fake. You see people pretending to believe that the other's illusionary mask fulfills life. You see this is empty power. If you see beyond that game, you won't become soft and loving immediately. Instead, you will use your power to avoid playing along. You reject it. You expose it and you announce the naked truth. This is new power, but it is more directed at yourself and less fearful than before. You can no longer be held back in your quest for the core, for the fulfillment of your need to touch.

Phase 2:
My Power Lies in the Knowledge of My Heart

Your longing to be together with others, to follow life instead of holding on to power, gets stronger. It is no longer taboo to be loving. You disarm. You glean strength from the realization that, on the inside, you are invulnerable. There is no power in the world that can control the person you are inside of you, even though you have not mastered the words to express it yet.

The next guardian stands in front of the next gate. It says, *"If you go on, you'll be all alone. Do you want to go through life like a pilgrim? You can't be like this in this society. You'll lose, and everybody will abandon you. Weren't you longing to be touched? Fall in line again and use this knowledge to become even more invulnerable!"*

Your inner strength will help you to pass this guardian. It is not bad to be alone, because you are filled with new life, even though you are still in the early stages. You are not truly alone, because you are in touch with yourself. Now, you have to learn to express yourself. Your old words don't suffice. Your old tone sounds too harsh. You are searching for your own tone. You open yourself up consciously, so that you are accessible to others. You begin to have a voice that others listen to, not because you give it extra power, but because on the inside you are sure of what you say. You speak from your heart to the individuality of the other. That is an entirely new kind of power. You have something to say, and you yourself are the proof of the truthfulness of your message. The secret you have discovered is that, in essence, the other is just as willing as you are to give up power and to be himself or herself. This is true brotherhood or sisterhood.

Yet the temptations of power have not completely vanished. Even though your newly found certainty is rooted in your heart, you are employing it to be with others. You can derive power from that anew, precisely because you know so well now what other people need and what they fear. For example, you could form a sect, or you could become a manager who knows what is good for his people or a therapist who is so understanding that his patients could not live without him. In a love relationship, you are the one who is fulfilling the other's existence. Actually, everything is possible now.

You do become tied down in this manner. You aren't really receptive, because you are directed at the wishes of others. If you don't watch out, you will get addicted to that. You trade in your freedom for the power to get in touch with others. You will notice this by not being truly receptive in your thoughts. You are not playing.

Phase 3:
The Other Has No Power over the One Who Has Become Completely and Totally Unique

A much deeper wish surfaces now, the wish to think completely from within yourself and to behave accordingly. You want to open your head to the light. The thoughts you are holding on to are like a prison, even though they are nourishment for the people around you.

The guardian shows itself again and says, *"Look, now you've figured it out. Everybody is happy. They really need you. If you don't watch them, they'll wander off. You accepted this responsibility and you should stick to it. Pressure is simply a part of it. That is the price you pay for brotherhood or sisterhood. If you walk on, nobody is going to follow you. And then what?"*

You pass by this guardian fully aware of the leap you are taking. With this, you truly give up all control of your time- and space-bound personality. You entrust yourself to your immortal center. You step into the emptiness. Your personality has become the pure expression of who you are. You are free and you sing back to life what life doesn't know yet.

Property—The Light Doesn't Belong to Anyone, It Plays Everywhere

One can't speak of an animal having possessions. An animal has and uses. Because of the urge to possess, an animal will do its utmost to get what it needs for its own survival and the survival of its family.

In this way, the urge to possess enables us to stand up for the things we cannot do without in our earthly existence. Because of the urge to possess, things are divided up in an orderly fashion—you are not wearing another's clothes, you are not writing in another's diary, you are not eating another's food. The urge to possess makes sure that we experience the difference between what is mine and yours energetically, as if it pertains to our bodies. When my purse is stolen, I literally experience that as if something is pulled from my body.

Just as was the case with sexuality and power, the urge to possess can become independent of its function. Then possessions are there to be possessed—there comes a lust to possess. Animals don't have that.

The important question is, What am I attached to, to what do I say *I*, what will I fight for as if my life depended on it? Our instincts are flexible. The more possessions we have, the more there is to be guarded, and the more our instincts will help us in that guarding. It is up to us how we want to use this instinct.

Phase 0:
I Have, Therefore I Am

While growing up, you form your own concept of *I*. Of course, in reality, everything you are is *I*—inside as well as outside. Our society, however, places a greater value on the visible part.

How do I look?

What good does it do you?

How well do you talk?

What can you do?

What all do you have?

How much does your father earn?

You keep growing, and that almost always means that you accumulate more: knowledge, skills, friends, work, money, things, a partner, kids, a philosophy. You can be very happy with them and keep on growing in a straight line. If you do, your *I* won't change much. Actually, it will continue as more of the same. Only what is on the outside increases.

In order to give in to the longing for adventure that might pop up once in a while, you can play video games or watch exciting movies or fly away. But even then, you are really just utilizing more possessions.

Phase 1:
How Boring Is Having

You may be happy to continue as you are until you notice that the urge to experience something new can never really be satisfied. There is always that carrot at the end of the stick. Something begins to gnaw at you, because, actually, you find life boring. No matter what happens, nothing ever seems to change. You begin to realize that you fill up on things to get rid of a boring gray feeling. You see that life will always be this way and that not a single material thing in this world can pull you out of it.

Now you are faced with a decision: take a bigger dose of the same or dare to leap, experiencing what will happen if you don't accumulate more. Here, too, is a guardian.

It knows the answer: *"You can do both. Aren't you allowed to enjoy all the good the earth has to offer? You aren't going to give it up for the chance to fall into a black hole that you will never get out of again, are you? And besides, what are people going to say?"*

Going beyond this guardian is the same as admitting that you don't know what you have in you. But you pass him precisely because you want to find out. That is very spooky. You are accustomed to seeking safety in filling up, and now you are going on toward a hollow emptiness. At the same time, you are admitting for the first time in your life that you need help. And somewhere inside, very deeply, there isn't emptiness. Something is moving. You feel that this is about the core. Something is beginning to move from within. You don't believe anymore that everything will always be the same. It is very difficult; sometimes life will be pitch-black, but no longer gray.

Phase 2: I Am

Of course, you won't be cured of your addiction to possessions immediately. The urge to take something is rooted too deeply. But you do recognize that the urge is there. You don't automatically give in to it anymore. You regard it more as a frustration now, an avoidance strategy, than a real wish. That is the beginning of detachment.

You begin to get in touch with the force that is set free the moment you no longer act automatically. Inside that force, there is something that knows what you need. You take your needs seriously, and you admit to them. You experience that you can trust yourself, that the well doesn't dry up immediately. You start to wonder who you really are.

Here, the next guardian shows up and says: *"Well, well. So you are, but you have nothing. Do you know what this is leading to? You'll have to let go of everything. You'll end up poor as a church*

*mouse and nobody will care for you. This is the path of destitution.
If you want to waste your strength on that, go ahead, but don't say
that I didn't warn you."*

If you don't shy away from this, you will complete this initiation. You are within the boundaries of your skin, and you are longing for the unification with the ever-giving source inside of you.

Now you have to learn to deal with your feelings, your wishes,
and your desires. In everyday life, it is possible that you lay yourself bare to somebody and that the response you get is rejection. It
is tempting then to leave it at that and to walk away from this new
frustration. Then life seems to be poverty, after all. Fulfillment is
apparently possible only if you adjust your wishes to the supply.

You don't have to close off despite all the pain—that is what this
is about. You become receptive. You learn to love people and you
learn to let go of people. You learn that the pain, once it has gone
through you, dissolves in a milder kind of love than you've ever
known before. This way, you begin to understand in your heart that
all is food. You accept life unconditionally. Slowly but gradually,
love is becoming a state of being. You are, and what you have is an
expression of that.

Phase 3: Not I

You have learned to transform the desire (more, more, more)
into love (being); you have learned not to follow your solar plexus,
but to follow the feelings of your heart. You also begin to notice that
there is something higher than "doing what feels good." How do
you notice? Because you long to enter a new realm.

Sometimes you feel caught in a loving environment, because
you can't spread your wings there. And if you are alone, you experience all kinds of thoughts that do not come from your heart. Love
isn't flowing. How do you let go of those thoughts, how do you

make the stream of love flow again? How do you become happy in your head?

The Bible says, "Man is as he thinks in his heart." This proverb becomes meaningful. How do you think in your heart? You begin to understand love as something different. It turns out to be a much more central experience; it is much more than the feeling that expresses itself in friendliness. Love is also engendered as a thought coming from the light. Such a thought comes into your head and your heart at the same time. If you follow it, you yourself generate the power of your tenderness.

Thus you begin to direct yourself toward the light. You learn to emote with your head. Is there light? Then you are surrounded by love. Is there darkness? Then you are mixing in your own *I*-directed thoughts. At this stage, it is not the desire for more that urges you on. No, you want to find yourself in nothingness by letting go of everything that could be "something."

Here again is the guardian. It says, *"You can't send me away. I will always think for you. I will always provide food for you. Now, after a lot of agony, you finally know what is good for you. Finally, life is good. You earned it, reap the harvest. Let me think for you now. You just rest."*

But you aren't looking for food anymore. You are at home in the emptiness. You are the one that continuously comes into being within it, in a continuous rebirth. To continue yourself in time, you don't have to possess anymore. You are who you are.

The third initiation is the setting free of possessions, power, and sex as independent powers. These three primal desires no longer govern the personality. This is the end of isolated existence, because you no longer use others to fulfill needs.

Father and mother—the great duality—have been given back to themselves. They aren't the cause of life and they don't determine the quality of life. Life gives birth to itself. The past is thankfulness now. The future is trust.

That is living in freedom—the basis of true unity.

ATTITUDE TOWARD	PARENTS
3rd Initiation: *Transfiguration* • Thoughts and wishes create a new reality • Becoming a cocreator	I give my parents back to themselves.
Mental Crisis Text of the Guardian: Phase 3: From the 2nd to the 3rd Initiation	You have to continue what already exists, otherwise things will go wrong. How could correct thoughts pop up inside of you just like that? No, you should never let go of a thought. Where are you going to go in this emptiness? Continue our work, so we can grow old in peace.
2nd Initiation: *Baptism* • Control of the emotional body and unification with the source of love • The astral becomes a mirror	I want to show myself to my parents.
Emotional Crisis Text of the Guardian: Phase 2: From the 1st to the 2nd Initiation	Your parents have shortcomings. You can't originate from within yourself in your relationshp to them. You have to close off your heart.
1st Initiation: *Birth* • The physical serves something bigger than the *I*. • Personality serves the soul.	I distance myself from my parents in the name of freedom.
Form Crisis Text of the Guardian: Phase 1: Trial Path	You're wrong. Everybody has short-comings. Nobody is absolutely good. You can't have everything you want.
From 0 to Trial Path:	Don't do this to us. We belong together. Nobody knows better than we what you need.
Phase 0: Old Trusty World	My parents are there for me.

SEXUALITY	POWER	PROPERTY
Light and pleasure become one.	The other has no power over the one who has become completely and totally unique.	Not I.
When you don't have me (my thoughts) anymore, there will be nothing left of you. I alone can guarantee your future. I am here and I will stay here, as always.	Look, now you've figured it out. Everybody is happy. They really need you. If you don't watch them, they'll wander off. You accepted this responsibility and you should stick to it. Pressure is simply a part of it. That is the price you pay for brotherhood/sisterhood. If you walk on, nobody is going to follow you. And then what?	I will always think for you. I will always provide food for you. Now, you finally know what is good for you. Finally, life is good. You earned it. Reap the harvest. Let me think for you now. You just rest.
The play becomes tender.	My power lies in the knowledge of my heart.	I am.
You aren't going to surrender to the unknown, are you? What are you going to do with all that longing? If you release that, it becomes much too strong. It will never be satisfied. Keep the lid on it!	If you go on, you'll be all alone. Do you want to go through life like a pilgrim? You can't be like this in this society. You'll lose, and everybody will abandon you. Weren't you longing to be touched? Fall in line again and use this knowledge to become even more invulnerable!	Well, well. So you are, but you have nothing. You'll end up poor as a church mouse and nobody will care for you. This is the path of destitution. If you want to waste your strength, go ahead, but don't say that I didn't warn you.
The child is allowed to play again.	What is that secret of contact?	How boring is having.
I warned you. What do you want with that flow? If you want to be somebody in this world, you should never let go. You should always think before you do.	Don't give in to that weakness. Do you want to live a boring life, with sweet whisperings, and that "I really need you" stuff? So you are like everybody else, after all? No more fun, that's the end of the game.	You can do both. Aren't you allowed to enjoy all the good earth has to offer? You aren't going to give it up for the chance to fall into a black hole that you will never get out of again, are you? And besides, what are people going to say?
Living in your head.	I have the power because nobody knows who I am.	I have, therefore I am.

Conclusion

You always leap alone. You cannot give up the illusion of the isolated *I* while together with others. You have to go alone, precisely because you are leaving your isolated being behind. You are breaking through your own separateness.

Of course it is possible—probable, even—that your friends and loved ones will take such a path too. You exchange ideas, and in that manner you support and help each other, insofar as one person can support another. But your resistance—your guardian—you meet alone. It is not the other's guardian. It is you, as you imagined yourself to be.

Initiation results when you no longer try to fill the emptiness with the structures of your personality. At the core of all things, at the core of existence, is an emptiness, a void, a mystery. When you allow the void to exist—not just in you, but also between you and the others—when you are able to endure the resulting tension, when you honor the silence, when you look at the other and do your daily duties, you will be admitted.

Then you will join a larger whole, and you will experience that all separate roads come together in one road. At the beginning, you could only suspect it.

You always leap alone. But coming down, you notice that you have joined hands.

Applied Integral Psychology

The meditation process in which, through self-knowledge (psychology), the separate bodies (physical, astral, mental, and causal) are distinguished, cleansed, and aligned (integral) in order to make concrete one's utmost knowledge and deepest desires (applied).

Archetypal Level

A level of humanness in which all individuals, groups, peoples, and races are rooted; the realm of common human themes. Myths and fairy tales emerge from this realm.

Astral Body (Emotional Body)

The unity of emotions and feelings, not generally visible but perceptible, made up of a finer and more far-reaching energy than the physical body; a condensing of the mental body.

Causal Body (Self)

The center of the human psyche, not subject to the influence of time. The one you are in essence, the soul, the source of your own thoughts and feelings as well as your physical body. The body that stretches out farthest and is composed of the finest energy.

Chakras

The connecting points between the various bodies; transformers that convert pure energy into specialized forms of energy that are necessary for various realms and phases of life. In *Inner Guidance,* we describe and distinguish between the following seven chakras: root chakra, sex chakra, solar plexus, heart chakra, throat chakra, forehead chakra, and crown chakra.

Character Structures

The materialized resistance of the personality, as manifested in the mental, astral, and physical bodies. In *Inner Guidance,* we distinguish and describe five character structures (following Wilhelm Reich, Alexander Lowen, and John Pierrakos): the schizoid structure, the oral structure, the masochist structure, the rigid structure, and the psychopathological structure.

Conservatism

The drive to regard as separate life's innumerable and related phenomena, and to permanently subsume them under one closed system.

Contraction Phase

The phase within the cycle of organic growth in which an inward turning takes place and in which experiences are processed.

Core Qualities

Expressions of the self, from which inspiration originates. They are the possibilities that man can tune in to as wavelengths from the world of thought, man being the receiver.

Crisis

Crisis arises when life surges toward the new and necessary changes are obstructed and denied. Crisis is a situation that one cannot perceive a way out of with one's three-dimensional consciousness; every emergency exit is closed, and one is faced with something insurmountable.

The word *crisis* literally means "turn around"; it is a renewed chance to allow in the new that was warded off until now. It is the letting go of old certainties and trusted patterns.

Crown Chakra

The center in the top of the head that is permanently directed at the reception of light. Here the person who has faced up to and accepted the darkest drives within himself, and who has subordinated them to the light, learns to detach himself from the darkness of his inner or outer world. He becomes a point of light himself.

Discipline

Choosing that which you love and, based on that, not fueling that which suits you less. Discipline requires an ability to perceive and distinguish objectively. One exercises discipline when one regards the impulses of thought as information and does not react emotionally to them.

Discrimination

The permanently condemnatory differentiation of one part of the whole by another part. There is no reciprocity, and it cannot arise.

Discrimination is a pseudo-solution that enables a herd to deal with its own undesirable tendencies, feelings, and thoughts. They are projected onto another herd and are then fought within that herd. In this fight the herd finds its self-affirmation, and it doesn't need to formulate a mature or personal answer to its own imperfections and negativity.

Distortions

When the personality does not serve the self, wants to stay in charge, and refuses to act as an instrument, core qualities turn into distortions. For example, flexibility becomes opportunism, and carefulness becomes fearful caution.

Duality

The splitting of a unity into opposites, such as day and night, warm and cold, or hard and soft.

Emotion

A stream of energy linked to the lower thought process that wants to be channeled and that, if undirected, will effectuate a tension in the organism.

Expansion Phase

A phase in the cycle of organic growth in which outward movement takes place and which is aimed at the discovery of the other and the new. In our present culture, this phase is equated with growth.

Feeling

An expression linked to natural knowledge, freely streaming and emanating by itself from the inside to the outside.

Forehead Chakra (Third Eye)

The center of the integrated personality, the gate for true self-knowledge. Seat of the power of visualization, the power to see immediately and to foresee latencies. Here, one learns to combine and to direct one's creative impulses.

Guardian of the Threshold

The figure that you meet in times of crisis at the threshold of a new realm you wish to enter, and who asks you to bring the necessary sacrifice. The personality projects all its resistance onto this figure so that it can avoid the sacrifice.

Heart Chakra

The center of love where egotism is transformed into selflessness, while climbing the ladder of consciousness and while preserving one's identity. Here, one learns how to liberate oneself from personal sympathies and antipathies in order to truly open oneself to the essence of the other and to form a bond with the other's essence.

Helpership

The assumption of the helper's function within the larger whole, in which you can express your essence to the maximum degree and in which you are maximally at home.

Herd

A collective with ideals aimed at the future. Herds always oppose other herds; a herd follows a shepherd who represents the ultimate authority. Herds are organized in a strict hierarchy that functions to subordinate personal opinions to the ideals of the collective.

Images

Personal opinions, presuppositions, and prejudices, either consciously or unconsciously held, that you allow to determine your life. They are unconscious conclusions stuck in your psyche that determine your actions without your being aware of it.

Individuation

The process in which you step out of the herd and regard yourself as the guide of your own life, when you don't allow yourself to be guided anymore by the answers of others but start searching actively for answers within yourself and, hence, for your own conscience. In this process, you discover your own qualities. It is the pursuit of your own path; you take the lead and assume the responsibility for your own life.

Initiation

Going beyond the impossibilities of your present level of consciousness to the next level of consciousness.

Instrument

The personality that chooses to serve the larger whole and take the path of surrendering, which happens when you entrust yourself to the guidance of the spirit that is expressed through the soul (or the causal body). When the personality takes this active path of surrendering, it becomes an instrument.

Karma

Everything you have to experience as a result of the direction you take with your energy in the various realms of being.

Ladder of Life

The seven great chakras are the stages on the road we take. In every chakra, heaven and earth meet in a person. In the lower three, the meetings occur in the earthly realm. In the top three chakras, they meet in the heavenly realm. Only in the fourth or middle chakra do the two streams meet without either one having an "advantage." At that stage, in the heart chakra, the great transition takes place. Many can actualize this transition in our times.

Leader

Somebody who is attuned to his or her core qualities and who places the personality in the service of the expression of these core qualities.

Mass

A collective in which no individual feelings, thoughts, and wishes exist. In order to belong to the mass, individuals have to act and think as the mass prescribes; they have to punish the deviant (scapegoats) and cheer the idols.

The mass is like an enormous amoeba that moves in waves. The waves are directed and legitimized by prejudices. These prejudices are called thoughts, but in reality, thoughts are free and prejudices are not.

Meditation

Everything you do to connect to your inner guiding principle. In particular, it is the distinguishing and "cleansing" of aspirations, feelings, and thoughts to attune them to the base tone of the soul.

Mental Body

The invisible, imperceptible, yet receivable unity of thoughts and ideas, made of even finer and even farther-reaching energy than the astral body.

Neurosis

A state of being in which you suppress your original needs; as a result, you lose touch with your deepest drives and your surroundings.

Personality

Derived from the Latin words *personare* (to be heard) and *persona* (stage mask). You relate to your surroundings through the personality. The personality as such is not a true center, but consists of many sub-personalities, each expressing itself in its own form. The integrated personality has harmonized thoughts and feelings and acts from that unity, contrary to the unintegrated personality, who is a toy of drives and of outside influences. In this book, we call the unintegrated personality the "isolated personality" or the "isolated *I*" or sometimes just the *I*.

Physical Body

The most concrete expression of the soul; a condensing of the astral body.

Projecting

To think of your own ideas of reality as reality itself.

Repression

The subconscious suppression of your wishes and impulses. Because of repression, you lose touch with these wishes and impulses, and hence they start leading their own lives in the psyche.

Root Chakra

The center of the will to live, where one totally connects to the earth from which one rose. If put in the service of the larger whole, this basic chakra allows one to enjoy all that is of the earth and the body, and to trust the energy of life rising up from the earth.

Sex Chakra

The center of physical creation and human reproductive power, where the great split takes place, but also the stage in which a union is possible from which new life can spring forth. Seat of lust and desire, where one learns to enjoy all aspects of life and where one is offered the final transformation opportunity to convert lustful desires into a longing of the soul for creative reproduction.

Solar Plexus

The center that houses the karma and the seat of the *I*-directed forces (like lust for power and self-preservation, and the fear of loss and demise). In this chakra, one learns to set and to deal with one's boundaries; in short, one learns to say *I*. The transformation opportunity offered here is to learn to entrust everything one has become to a higher guidance: the voice that speaks from the next center, the heart chakra.

Soul

The one you essentially are (see also *causal body*).

Static Phase

The phase within the cycle of organic growth in which "being" is experienced. There is silence and motionlessness.

Thought Apparatus (Linear or Lower Thinking)

The instrument serving human beings as a reservoir of information and as the faculty of weighing and combining various data. It knows how to make causal links and how to anticipate the future based on past experiences.

Throat Chakra

The center of the creative power, directly linked to the sex chakra. Here, the individualized person (solar plexus) who has found himself as an integral part of and as an expression of love (heart) becomes a (co-) creator of life.

Transference

The automatic application of past experiences with authority figures to present situations; transference can be either negative or positive.

Transference is negative when you assume that the authority figure is evil and punitive and has nothing good in store for you. Transference is positive when you assume that the authority figure is good, does not make mistakes, and will help and protect you in any way possible.

Positive transference is not really positive. It is a form of negative transference that appears to be good, as is apparent when, after a while, the authority figure falls off his or her pedestal.

Countertransference happens when an authority figure responds to the wishes and demands coming out of transference.

$\mathscr{B}ibliography$

We list here a number of books that had a fundamental influence on our lives and that greatly contributed to the writing of this book. Each of us selected six of our favorite books to include in the list. We chose not to include generally known works, such as the Bible or *Grimms' Fairy Tales*.

Alder, Vera Stanley. *The Initiation of the World*. London: Rider, 1968.

The author explains the relationship between age-old wisdom and contemporary scientific knowledge in an enjoyable and clear manner.

Bailey, Alice. *The Rays and the Initiations*. Vol. 5 of *A Treatise on the Seven Rays*. New York: Lucius, 1951–62.

Before a person can enter the path, he has to become that path.
As with most books by Alice Bailey, this one demands a lot of the reader. If you like Bailey's writing style and manner of thinking, your efforts will be rewarded richly. The book offers a trove of information about the path of initiation.

Buber, Martin. *Die chassidische Botschaft* (The Hasidic Message). Heidelberg: Lambert Schneider, 1952.

This book describes in a mythical, profound, and loving way the journey from duality to unity.

Canetti, Elias. *Crowds and Power*. Translated by Carol Stewart. New York: Farrar, Straus & Giroux, 1984 (c1962).

This book offers an excellent description of kinds of groups and the formations of power that govern them. Observations of everyday life in all times are explained and classified in a thorough manner. Required reading for politicians.

Card, Orson Scott. *Spreker voor de doden* (Speaker for the Dead). Amsterdam: Meulenhoff, 1988.

Describes very subtly, and in a way that can be identified with completely, the relationship between humankind and a nonhuman race. The main protagonist committed a horrible crime in his past (see the book *Ender's Game* [Amsterdam: Meulenhoff, 1989; New York: Doherty, 1985]). He has forgiven himself and has become a master who can speak with total inner conviction about a deceased person, enabling the survivors to carry him in their hearts as he really was.

Charon, Jean E. *Le monde eternel des eons.* Paris: Stock, 1980.

"Let me explain to you how I, just like all of you, live my eternal life." The author starts from the principle that the kernel of our powers is in the smallest particle our bodies are made of: the eon. These are elements in every human being that have lived for billions of years. He offers a clear, simple, and imaginative explanation of how henceforth the psyche and the spirit are part of the realm of the sciences.

Chuang Tzu. *The Complete Works of Chuang Tzu.* Translated by Burton Watson. New York: Columbia University Press, 1968.

Chuang Tzu constantly tricks you out of the beliefs you most want to hold on to. He is a great sage who never stops laughing.

Dass, Ram, and Paul Gorman. *How Can I Help?* London: Rider, 1985.

A beautiful booklet, full of real-life examples of people helping other people. Very natural, humorous, and touching.

Dickson, Gordon. *The Final Encyclopedia.* New York: Berkeley Publishing Group, Ace Science Fiction Books, 1985.

"All his life until this moment, it had been easier to imagine the death of the universe than his own. But now, at last, his personal mortality had become as real to him as the walls enclosing him. His end could only be a handful of hours away, unless something—some miracle—could prevent it."

This book describes in great detail the positive and negative consequences of super-specialization. The main theme is the battle between good and evil, but as it turns out, the two are "brothers in battle." To find solutions, one has to go back to an undifferentiated state of being.

Govinda, Lama Anagarika. *Foundations of Tibetan Mysticism.* London: Rider, 1969.

A book about Tibetan Buddhism, in which experience and wisdom come together. A wise book, useful for study and a delight to read. Govinda describes himself as "a citizen of India of European descent, a Buddhist belonging to a Tibetan Order and believing in the Brotherhood of Man."

I Ching: The Book of Changes. Translated by John Blofeld. London: Allen and Unwin, 1965.

The basis of this book goes back to the legendary emperor Fu Hsi in 3000 B.C. It is one of the oldest books in the world. The foundation of Chinese philosophy, it is a book of oracles and wisdom offering many clear directions for the practice of everyday life.

Kaiser, J. W. *Gebooretweeën van de nieuwe mens* (Birthing Pangs of the New Man). The Hague: Servire, n.d.

Everything written by Kaiser is valuable. Radical in his messages, old-fashioned in his language, brusque in his tone, he writes as if chopping his words in the reader's resistance. The lover of fairy tales will find great delight in his debut book, *Fairy Tale Wisdom* (The Hague: Servire, 1964).

Lao Tzu. *The Tao Te Ching: A New Translation with Commentary.* Translated by Ellen M. Chen. New York: Paragon, 1989.

Lao Tzu, the elder contemporary of Confucius, was an imperial archivist in Hunan Province in the sixth century B.C. Throughout his life he taught, "The Tao that can be spoken is not the eternal Tao." Nevertheless, he wrote down his insights. Legend has it that he rode off into the desert to die, disgusted by the way people behaved, when he was overtaken by a gatekeeper in northwestern China and was persuaded to preserve his insights for posterity. The eighty-one chapters of the book contain the essence of Taoism.

Meyrink, Gustav. *The Angel of the West Window.* Translated by Mike Mitchell. Riverside, Calif.: Ariadne Press, 1991.

This is Gustav Meyrink's (1868–1932) last and best novel. It is a well-written, suspenseful initiation novel. Every time one reads it, there is something new to be found. An excellent cast of "servants of evil": the pantherlike queen Assja Chotokalungin, the dubious antiquarian Lipotin, the laboratory assistant Kelley with his cut-off ears, the brute Bartlett Green, sympathic despite his brutality, and the horrifying angel. What reader could ever forget him! Beautiful imagery. An entanglement of intrigue leads to a conclusion where "lead" is turned into "gold," darkness into light.

Nisargadatta, Maharaj. *Zelf-realisatie.* Compiled by Robert Powell. Hilversum: Uitgeverij Altamira, 1988.

Sri Nisargadatta is a master teacher and destroyer of thought systems. He is loving and crystal clear. Anybody who engages in him—who reads the words he spoke—will either open himself up or not. This has nothing to do with Sri Nisargadatta. He is free.

Sturgeon, Theodore. *More than Human.* New York: Ballantine Books, 1989.

Almost all books written by Sturgeon are worth reading. This author, who died in 1986, inspires the reader through his language, his deeply human insights, and his extraordinary powers of observation.

Trungpa, Chogyam. *Meditation in Action.* London: Stuart and Watkins, 1969.

An excellent aid for anyone wanting to learn how to meditate. Trungpa takes you by the hand by telling what purpose meditation serves and how you can deal in a very practical manner with the obstructions you'll find on your path.

———. *De mythe van vrijheid* (The Myth of Freedom and the Way of Meditation). Katwijk aan Zee: Servire, 1989.

Written in a clear language indicative of the high mountains of Tibet, the book is a journey through the sense and senselessness of our lives—a difficult journey that leads to clarification without losing love and shows us the nonsense without losing humor. This is thinking in the highest octave.

Works Cited

Bailey, Alice. *Glamour: A World Problem.* New York: Lucis, 1967. (My translation.)

———. *Initiation, Human and Solar.* New York: Lucis, 1922. (My translation.)

The Bhagavad Gita. Translated with a general introduction by Eknath Easwaran and chapter introductions by Diana Morrison. Tomales, Calif.: Nilgiri Press, 1985.

The Bhagavadgita. With an introductory essay, Sanskrit text, English translation and notes by S. Radhakrishnan. Bombay: Allen and Unwin, 1971.

Buber, Martin. *The Legend of the Baal-Shem.* Translated by Maurice S. Friedman. New York: Harper, 1955.

Dam, Betty van. *Op zoek naar je levensenergie* (In Search of One's Energy of Life), in tijdschrift De Ketting, juli 1989. (My translation.)

Fentener van Vlissingen, R. *Ondergang en verheffing* (Downfall and Elevation). The Hague: Boucher, 1962. (My translation.)

Freitag, K. E. *Het lied van de parel.* Amsterdam: Theosofische Uitgeverij, n.d. (My translation.)

Govinda, Lama Anagarika. *The Way of the White Clouds: A Buddhist Pilgrim in Tibet.* London: Hutchinson, 1966.

Grimm, Jacob, and Wilhelm Grimm. *The Complete Fairy Tales of the Brothers Grimm.* Translated and with an introduction by Jack Zipes. New York: Bantam, 1987.

Heindel, Max, and Augusta Foss Heindel. *Astrologie* (The Message of the Stars). Amsterdam: Querido, 1955. (My translation.)

The Holy Bible. Revised Standard Version. New York: Nelson, 1952.

Kafka, Franz. "Before the Law." Translated by Willa and Edwin Muir. In *The Penguin Complete Short Stories of Franz Kafka*. Edited by Nahum N. Glatzer. Harmondsworth: Penguin Books, 1983.

Kaiser, J. W. *De mysteriën van Jezus in ons leven*. The Hague: Servire, 1965. (My translation.)

—————. *Geboorteweeën van de nieuwe mens* (Birthing Pangs of the New Man). The Hague: Servire, n.d. (My translation.)

Kerényi, Karl. *Eleusis, de heiligste mysteriën van Griekenland* (Eleusis: The Most Sacred Mysteries of Greece). The Hague: Servire, 1960.

Korteweg, Hans, and Jaap Voigt. *Helen of delen: transformatie van mens en organisatie* (Healing or Dividing). Amsterdam: Contact, 1986.

Korteweg-Frankhuisen, Hanneke, and Hans Korteweg. *Innerlijke leiding: de kunst om de innerlijke stem te volgen tot in de dagelijkse praktijk* (Inner Guidance). Katwijk aan Zee: Servire, 1989.

Lilly, John. *The Center of the Cyclone: An Autobiography of Inner Space*. New York: Julian Press, 1972.

Loon, Corrie van, and Hans Korteweg. *Echt waar: wensen worden werkelijkheid* (Really True: Wishes Do Come True). Deventer: Ankh Hermes, 1987. (My translation.)

Lytton, Edward Bulwer. *Zanoni*. Vol. 8 of *Lord Lytton's Works*. New York: International, n.d.

Mahy, Margaret. *De inwijding* (The Initiation). Amsterdam: Querido, 1987. (My translation.)

Meyrink, Gustav. *The Green Face*. Translated by Mike Mitchell. Riverside, Calif.: Ariadne Press, 1992.

Nossack, Hans Erich. *Spirale: Roman einer schlaflosen Nacht*. Frankfurt: Suhrkamp, 1956.

————. *Unmögliche Beweisaufnahme* (The Impossible Proof). Frankfurt: Suhrkamp, 1959. (My translation.)

————. *Der Untergang* (The Demise). Frankfurt: Suhrkamp, 1948. (My translation.)

Ouspensky, Petr Demianovich. *De mens en zijn mogelijke evolutie* (The Psychology of Man's Possible Evolution). Katwijk aan Zee: Servire, 1988. (My translation.)

Reps, Paul. *Zen Flesh, Zen Bones: A Collection of Zen and Pre-Zen Writing.* Rutland: Tuttle, 1957.

Rilke, Rainer Maria. *The Book of Images.* Bilingual edition. Translated by Edward Snow. San Francisco: North Point Press, 1991.

Sophocles. *The Theban Plays: King Oedipus, Oedipus at Colonus, Antigone.* Translated by E. F. Watling. Harmondsworth: Penguin Books, 1974.